SEARCHING FOR THE PALACE
OF ODYSSEUS

An ancient head of the blind poet Homer. There are good reasons for suggesting that he was indeed blind. The evidence for this is given in the text. This depiction of the blind Homer is preserved at Munich. It is a Roman copy from the early Imperial period of a bronze Greek statue dating from circa 450 BC. The photo is reproduced from Karl Schefold, *Die Bildnisse der Antiken Dichter Redner und Denker* (*The Likenesses of Ancient Poets, Orators, and Thinkers*), Benno Schwabe & Co. Verlag, Basel, Switzerland, 1943, p. 63.

SEARCHING FOR THE PALACE OF ODYSSEUS

by

Robert Temple

eglantyne books

Published by Eglantyne Books ltd,
The Club Room, Conway Hall, 25 Red Lion Square, London WC1R 4RL.
www.eglantynebooks.com
©2023 by Robert Temple.
ISBN 978-1-913378-17-2
Printed in the UK by Imprint Digital ltd.
A CIP record for this title is available from the British Library.
Book layout and design by Eric Wright
Production team:
Robert and Olivia Temple, Michael Lee and Eric Wright

The Odyssey by Homer is one of the great works of world literature. It deals with the wanderings and eventual return home of Odysseus after the end of the Trojan War (12ᵗʰ or 13ᵗʰ century BC, the 'Mycenaean Period'). Did a man named Odysseus really exist? Or was he made up by Homer? And if so, did he really come from the Greek island of Ithaca (now called Ithaki in modern Greek)? Was he really its king as Homer said? If so, he must have had one of those typical Mycenaean palaces which are so familiar to archaeologists, and some excavated ones of which can also be seen by the public. But because Ithaca was a remote place and a small island, the Palace of Odysseus would have been smaller than some of the grander palaces known on the mainland of Greece. However, such was the standardisation of design at that time in Greek history, we can be certain of its general shape and its layout. Greek palaces at that time were all basically the same, differing only in size and in such details as whether the womens' quarters were, say, at the side or at the rear of the palace. We will be learning more about these details later on, and examining what Homer himself said about the physical details of the Palace of Odysseus. For Homer was very exact in his descriptions, so much so that one has the eerie feeling that he must have known such a palace, even though they had ceased to exist hundreds of years before his time. But there is a solution to that enigma which, as we shall see, is rather unexpected.

As a small archaeometric (dating) team, my wife Olivia and I visited Ithaca and looked for the site of the Palace with our colleague Professor Ioannis Liritzis of the University of the Aegean. Ioannis had been a nuclear physicist before changing to archaeology, and he has invented a novel archaeological dating technique. It is able to date when two pieces of stone have been pressed together in the process of construction, in other words, when the stones were actually used to construct something. The basis of this is the dating of tiny samples by complex scientific means in laboratories so as to reveal when those surfaces were last exposed to light. The technique is explained later. The technique is known as *optical thermoluminescence*, and is not the same as *thermoluminescence*, which is well known and constantly used in archaeology.

As a result of our efforts, we believe we have found the original site of the Palace of Odysseus, the hero of Homer's *Odyssey*. We have verified the date of the site as Mycenaean by Ioannis's dating technique, which is described later. This is the period which included the Trojan War. We may therefore have found the home of one of the most famous men in the history of Western civilisation, Odysseus, who is also often known by his Roman name of Ulysses.

Many, if not most, scholars have believed that a man named Odysseus really existed, and that Odysseus was not just the name of an imaginary character in a heroic poem. Of course, the question as to whether the real historical Odysseus had all the adventures described in Homer's *Odyssey* is another matter. Undoubtedly he did not! But there is a high probability that a real person named Odysseus existed, fought at Troy, returned home after a long time to Ithaca, and gave his name to the semi-legendary character in the Homeric epic which was named the *Odyssey* after him. His homecoming to Ithaca is likely to have been a real event, whereas the visits to Circe, Calypso, the Lotus Eaters, the Cyclops, the Sirens, and the other magical adventures of the epic were obviously literary fictions.

The story of the *Odyssey* tells of the time after the end of the Trojan War, when the Greeks in their many separate boats returned to their homes in Greece after being away for so many years. Odysseus was one of the chief Greek personages fighting at Troy. He came from the Island of Ithaca, off the west coast of Greece. He is variously described in different sources either as the King of Ithaca or as the King of Cephallonia, the larger island which is opposite Ithaca. It seems that the three adjoining islands, Cephallonia, Ithaca, and Leukas, formed a single kingdom, so that Odysseus could be described either as King of Ithaca or King of Cephallonia, since both really meant the same thing. But Ithaca seems to have been his actual place of residence within the three isles.

The epic then tells of the struggles of Odysseus over many years to return to his homeland, and the many harrowing adventures he had on the way. Finally, he reaches Ithaca and plots how to return to his palace unmolested. He is many years older, and is dressed as a vagabond so that no one would recognise him upon first approach. In fact, only his old dog Argos recognises him. He comes to realize just how dire the situation at his palace really is. His wife Penelope lives in the palace, but hordes of men from various places are camping there and essentially besieging her. They are constantly fighting amongst themselves and pressuring her to marry one of them. It is obvious that he will have to fight them and defeat them all, in order to regain his rightful place, his wife, and his palace.

Just in case anyone is deeply puzzled at the fact that for many years during Odysseus's absence Penelope was surrounded by suitors, it should be made clear that it was not necessarily because men lusted after women in her position that they wanted them, but because in ancient Greece, women who were heiresses were the transmitters of property from one man (a father, brother, or deceased husband) to another. Such a woman in hand was therefore like a deed of property and a bank account combined, if you could seize her or persuade her. This has been well documented for classical Athens, where an heiress who was already married with children could be legally seized by a cousin as his wife, in order to transmit the family property to himself, revoking her previous marriage and dragging her from her own home. Such things actually happened! This was all elucidated by Charles Albert Savage in his seminal book *The Athenian Family: A Sociological and Legal Study*.[1] He states that a wife was 'merely an instrument or a piece of machinery in the inheritance system'.[2] He was speaking of Athenian law. But it appears by inference that in Mycenaean Greece, the role of the woman as transmitter was extended beyond mere property, and included transmission of a kingship as well. If one of the suitors could have obtained Penelope as a wife, he would not only own the Palace of Odysseus as a result, but would also become the new King of the Ithacans in place of Odysseus's son Telemachos, whom they intended to murder. These legal implications of the ancient epic tales seem never to have been considered by scholars. They raise interesting questions about the nature of Mycenaean kingship in general, and its relationship to palace ownership. But these are issues for social historians of Mycenaean Greece, if there are any.

Plate 1. The head of a woman of the Archaic Period in Greece, preserved at the Acropolis Museum in Athens. Penelope might well have been such a classic beauty. Reproduced from Charles Diehl, *Excursions in Greece*, London, 1893, p. 113.

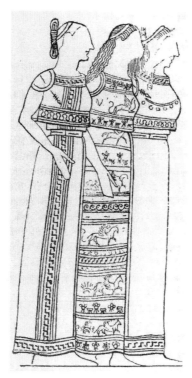

Figure 1. This sixth century BC image of three women in embroidered dress (each is wearing a garment called a Doric peplos) has featured in scholarly discussions of Penelope's attire, primarily because the woman on the left has a clearly visible straight pin at her collar bone, with the pin head pointing downward, which holds the dress together. Penelope on the other hand would have worn a peplos with an opening down the front, which would have been fastened in the front by some other means, and not by a straight pin in the manner shown here. Detail drawn from the Francois Vase in the Archaeological Museum in Florence. The vase is Etruscan, and dates from circa 570-560 BC. Reproduced from H. L. Lorimer, *Homer and the Monuments*, Macmillan, London, 1950, p 379, Fig. 54.

It is worth noting that there was a variant version of a related epic called *The Telegony* cited in surviving fragments of a lost work by Aristotle, and that it was a version which Aristotle personally found in the Ionian Islands (of which Ithaca is one), giving a version of the story which was probably closer to the original intention of the author, and possibly closer to any possible historical facts upon which the story may have been based, with a distinct Ithacan slant. This has been explained at length by W. R. Halliday, who writes:

'The version, then, which Aristotle was following, is markedly different not only from Homer but from the Cyclic tradition, and a feature of it seems to be a relatively local interest. The places and persons belong to North-Western Greece and its islands. … Now that a local version of the story of Odysseus existed [at Ithaca] which differed from the epic tradition precisely in respect of the localization of persons and characters in the vicinity of Ithaka, and further that it was known to Aristotle, seems to be shown by *Poetics*, xxv, 16, 1461b.'[3] In fact, Aristotle records the fact that the wife of Odysseus, Penelope, was not Spartan as most people thought, but was really from Odysseus's kingdom of Cephallonia (which included Ithaca), and this is substantiated by a remark written in the margin of an old manuscript of the *Odyssey* by a scholar of the type called a 'scholiast' (the word used for ancient commentators, who usually wrote in margins).

Plate 2. Ithaca before the modern tourist age was still a traditional place, and relatively isolated. Here we see two of the local inhabitants in the mountains of Ithaca in the 1920s. (Reproduced from Plate II of Alexander Shewan, 'Ithaka', in *Antiquity*, Vol. I, No. 4, December, 1927, opposite p. 408.)

As for the *Odyssey* itself, as it was known to Aristotle, he mentions nowhere in the *Poetics* anything about the fantasy elements of the epic, but he prefers to refer to it as if it were a pure *Return of Odysseus*. He even stresses the fact that the epic only contains two themes, the tragedy of Odysseus and the tragedy of the suitors:

'The argument of the *Odyssey* is not a long one. A certain man has been abroad many years; Poseidon is ever on the watch for him, and he is all alone. Matters at home too have come to this, that his substance is being wasted and his son's death is plotted by suitors to his wife. Then he arrives there himself after his grievous sufferings; reveals himself, and falls on his enemies; and the end is his salvation and their death. This being all that is proper to the *Odyssey*, everything else in it is episode.'[4]

Figure 2. Here is an Etruscan depiction of Odysseus's wife Penelope raising her hand in a gesture of protest and rejection to two of her suitors at Ithaca, during the long absence of her husband. This image occurs on the reverse side of an Etruscan mirror preserved in the Museum of the Collegio Romano. Reproduced from Eduard Gerhard, *Etruskische Spiegel (Etruscan Mirrors)*, Berlin, 1867, Volume IV, Plate CDV. *(Collection of Robert Temple)*

But this extensive subject is too far from our concerns here, as we must now turn our attention more specifically to the Palace of Odysseus on Ithaca. Further discussions of the various texts is to be found at the end of the book.

There were people living on Ithaca over many centuries who claimed direct descent from the swineherd of Odysseus named Eumaois, or Eumaeus. In the *Odyssey*, he helps his old master defeat the suitors and regain his palace. These 'descendants of Eumaeus', or Coliadae as they called their clan, are very important, as we shall see a little later on, since they were in charge of the Ithacan shrine called the Odysseion, where the spirit of Odysseus was worshipped as a demi-god for hundreds of years. And they provided

11

the ancient tourist guides which I suggest in a moment were known to Homer. It seems evident that Aristotle must have encountered a later generation of these same people on a visit to Ithaca, and discussed them and their claims of descent from Eumaeus in his lost book entitled *Homeric Problems*.

Plate 3. The ruins of the Odysseion shrine, where Odysseus was worshipped as a demi-god (*hero*) at the foot of the small cliff, which is the edge of the hill where the Palace was. The Mycenaean stairway leading up to the site of the Palace is behind and to the right of the camera (see Plate 20). A preliminary excavation of this site has been undertaken by Greek archaeologists, as may be seen here. *(Photo by Robert Temple)*

Odysseus was worshipped as a hero even in ancient Laconia (Lacadaemonia, the capital of which was Sparta). As Farnell tells us in his book *Greek Hero Cults & Ideas of Immortality*:

'(He) was worshipped in Laconia purely as a hero and as the husband of Penelope, who was of Laconian family: and in the account of the cult given us by Plutarch we see the influence of the Homeric and post-Homeric epics; and again in the establishment of his worship on the coast of Libya, in the territory identified with the land of the Lotophagoi [Lotus Eaters]. Also, the frequent mention in the *Odyssey* of Odysseus's intercourse with the people of the mainland opposite his island will explain the record, for which we are indebted to Aristotle, that an Aetolian tribe, the Eurutanai, paid him heroic honours and consulted his shrine for purposes of divination, calling it "the oracle of Odysseus".'[5]

It is ironical that Odysseus was worshipped in Laconia on the premise that his wife was Laconian, considering that she was really Cephallonian and never set foot in Laconia in her life, as Aristotle discovered, and as I have recounted above. But sometimes any excuse to grab a celebrity will do. Maybe the Spartans thought they needed to spice up their public relations.

There were many more works of literature written about Odysseus, including several plays by famous Athenian dramatists, all of which are lost. And some of the fragments of these works preserve fascinating information. It was the tyrant Peisistratus of Athens (who ruled 546 BC – 527/8 BC) who made the first serious and extensive efforts to collect and compile definitive editions of Homeric texts. In his time, they were still recited and not read, as this fragment of an ancient life of Homer makes clear by referring to their 'performance':

'And his [Homer's] true poems, which were previously *performed* [my italics] in a scattered way, were collected by Peisistratus of Athens, as the following epigram inscribed on the statue of Peisistratus himself in Athens shows.'[6]

But we cannot discuss the ancient Odyssean literary tradition further here, and must turn our attention to our specific findings about the Palace of Odysseus itself.

The site of the Palace of Odysseus is at Pelicata [*Pelikata*], at the northern end of the island of Ithaca (*Ithaka, known today in modern Greek as Īthakī*). This location is shown in the map in Figure 3. From this elevated site, one can see three seas, as claimed in ancient literature, and as discussed later.

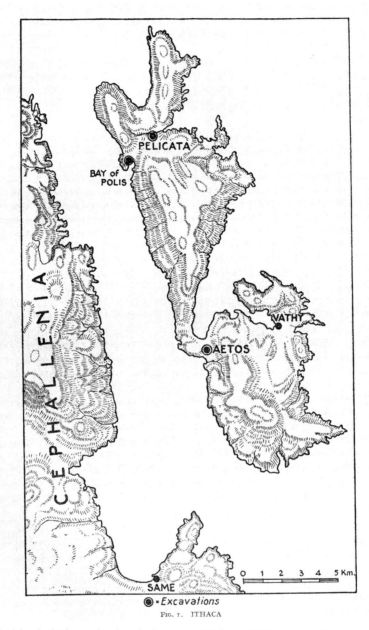

Figure 3. Map of the island of Ithaca, showing the location of Pelicata (Pelikata). near the northern end of the island. (Reprinted from *Antiquity*, 1935)

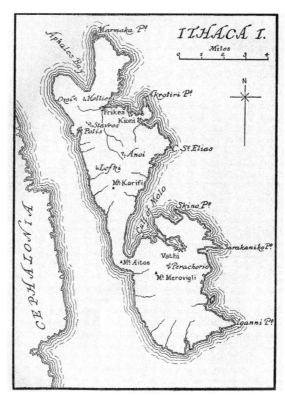

Figure 4. Map of the Island of Ithaca showing modern place names. The site of the Palace of Odysseus, at Pelikata (not shown), is near Stavros, between Polis and Frikes, and overlooks the Bay of Polis. (Reproduced from Alexander Shewan, 'Ithaka', in *Antiquity*, Vol. I, No. 4, December, 1927, p. 403.)

At the foot of the cliff modern excavations have revealed a site much used for centuries from the Archaic through the Hellenistic eras as a shrine, which was evidently the *Odysseion* of Ithaca, or the site of the semi-divine hero Odysseus who was worshipped here in later ages, many centuries after the end of the Mycenaean civilisation.

The palace itself has disappeared, although foundations presumably lie below the surface and require excavation. Visible above the surface today are parts of the original circuit wall of the palace precinct and an impressive old stone stairway going up a small cliff and leading to the site of the actual palace. We have dated this ancient stairway, as mentioned later.

This site at Pelicata has been the subject of much speculation as a possible site of the Palace of Odysseus for many decades, and some of the crucial evidence for the palace which existed in the 1930s has now vanished, such as the Mycenaean dressed stone blocks to be seen in the old photo reproduced as Plate 4.

Plate 4. In 1934, these dressed stone blocks which W. E. Heurtley believed to be of Mycenaean date, were still sitting on the site of the Palace of Odysseus. Since that time, they have all been taken away by the local people and re-used for their own walls and construction purposes, so that this important evidence for the ancient palace has vanished. However, it might be possible to trace some of them by making local enquiries. (*British School of Archaeology at Athens, reprinted from Antiquity*)

The local inhabitants have evidently helped themselves to these stones as they did in earlier times to a vast number of others. This is very much a Greek tradition. For instance, the largest petrified forest in Europe was once to be seen at the western end of the island of Lesbos. It was the inspiration for the treatise *On Things Which Have Turned to Stone* by Theophrastus of Eresos (c. 370 BC – 287 BC), the successor of Aristotle, whose parental home was a short distance (approximately a two-hour donkey ride) from the stone forest. But I have personally seen more petrified trees in the private homes of the local residents than can now be seen in situ. Much of the Palace of Odysseus on Ithaca also still survives, but in the form of blocks in walls and houses and as elements shoring up the agricultural terraces of the hillside. Rural Greece is a thrifty place, where everything has to be recycled. A Greek farmer cannot let a good stone go to waste, he must carry it away, just as the farmers of Wiltshire in England carried away most of the Avebury megaliths in the 18th and 19th centuries.

The most emphatic and insistent article suggesting the possibility of the Palace of Odysseus having once existed at Pelicata was published by W. A. Heurtley, of the British School of Archaeology at Athens, in 1935. This appeared in the British archaeological journal *Antiquity*.[7] Heurtley carried out some excavations at the site (apparently in 1934, though he does not mention the dates) on behalf of the British School and discovered a considerable amount of Mycenaean material. His account is of fundamental importance and a landmark in the study of this subject, especially as we regard our dating work as confirming Heurtley's earlier hypothesis.

Plate 5. Dr. W. A. Heurtley of the British School of Archaeology at Athens standing in front of the ancient circuit wall of the Palace of Odysseus in 1934. He found many Mycenaean remains in the immediate vicinity and strongly suspected that this was the location of the Palace, which we have at last been able to confirm with our dating results. (*British School of Archaeology at Athens. Reprinted from Antiquity*)

Plate 6. Robert Temple (left) and Professor Ioannis Liritzis on our first joint visit to the site of the Palace of Odysseus on the island of Ithaca. We are standing in front of the ancient circuit wall of the Palace precincts, below the slope with the ancient Mycenaean steps leading up to the Palace itself. We are in precisely the spot where Dr. W. A. Heurtley of the British School of Archaeology at Athens stood in 1934, as seen in Plate 6. (*Photo by Olivia Temple*)

Plate 7. Heurtley's photo of the remains of part of the ancient circuit wall, of which the lowest course is original and the upper part is modern. (*British School of Archaeology at Athens. Reprinted from Antiquity*)

Heurtley commences by saying:

'Many Homeric scholars who believe that modern Ithaca is the Ithaca of the *Odyssey* have selected the hill of Pelicata in the north of the island for the site of the palace of Odysseus. Apart from considerations of Homeric topography, it is, in fact, the one spot in Ithaca which, on the analogy of the Mycenaean sites elsewhere, strikes the eye immediately as suitable for a Mycenaean prince's citadel. It is sufficiently high; from its summit a ship entering any of the three harbours at the north end of the island can be seen; yet it is sufficiently distant from them all to be secure from any sudden attack by pirates.'[8]

When Heurtley speaks of those 'scholars who believe that modern Ithaca is the Ithaca of the *Odyssey*', he is referring to the theories put forward by a variety of people that the islands round the modern Ithaca have all changed their names in a kind of reshuffle. I have in my library a book devoted to the theory that Cephallonia is really the ancient Ithaca, but I have to say that the book is remarkably unconvincing, so I shall not bother to cite it. Others such as the German scholar Dörpfeld have tried to suggest that the island now known as Leucas [*spelled in modern Greek Leukada and pronounced Lefkada*], to the north of modern Ithaca, is the ancient Ithaca. But I do not believe any of these wild theories. I think Ithaca is Ithaca. Trying to change that is an act of desperation! We certainly know that by the second century AD, Ithaca was most definitely *not* identified with Cephallonia, since Plutarch mentions Cephallonia, Ithaca, and Zakinthos together in one sentence as three separate islands.[9]

However, one can appreciate the reasons for the desperation, for many scholars expected the real Ithaca to have a wonderful palace, and since they couldn't find it, the island must be wrong! Then after Heurtley published his article in 1935, few people took any notice of it, and speculation continued to run amok that Ithaca was somewhere else, even though Heurtley had pointed very clearly to a possible site of the missing palace, and had excavated many objects there of Mycenaean date.

In 1932, only three years before the appearance of Heurtley's article, the desperation of the situation was summed up by Martin Nilsson:

'Odysseus has his home on Ithaca, and the scene of the greater part of the *Odyssey* is laid on that island. Since the search for Mycenaean remains according to the guidance of the Homeric myths had been rewarded so brilliantly at Mycenae and at Troy, it is intelligible that Mr. Schliemann planned and Professor Dörpfeld attempted to carry out the plan to discover Odysseus' palace on Ithaca. Of course Professor Dörpfeld holds the opinion that old Ithaca was in reality Leucas. We need not discuss that vexed question here. On both islands the search for Mycenaean remains failed, generally speaking; all that was found were some few sherds such as appear even in countries distant from Greece. [*As we now know, only two years later, plenty of Mycenaean remains would be found at Pelicata by Heurtley.*] ... apart from the story of his return, Odysseus is one of the most prominent Homeric heroes and plays a most important part in the *Iliad*. That seems to prove that he, as well as other heroes, belonged to the old stock. His very name shows signs of great antiquity. The ending is the one common in the earlier stratum of heroic names, *-eus*, and the varying forms, Odysseus, Olytteus, etc., present a perplexing philological problem and prove the ancient origin of the name; for later names are regularly so formed that their origin is clear.

'Odysseus lived at Ithaca, be it the historical Ithaca, or Leucas. Although he himself plays a very prominent part in the *Iliad*, his country and his people are mentioned only twice. In the rather late scene where Helen from the walls of Troy points out the Greek heroes to the Trojans, she says that he was bred in the rocky country of Ithaca [III, 5, 201]; and in another place the herald Eurybates is said to be an Ithacan [II, 5, 184]. On the other hand, when Odysseus' people are mentioned in the mustering of the troops by Agamemnon, they are said to be Cephallenians [i.e., the Cephallonians; IV, 5, 330]. In the *Odyssey* Odysseus lives on Ithaca and is twice called an Ithacan, but he is not called king of Ithaca but king of the Cephallenians. This occurs in the late narrative of his meeting with his old father Laërtes [*Odyssey*, XXIV, 5, 350]. He fears that the Ithacans may send messages to the towns of the Cephallenians. Remembering the prowess of his youth, Laërtes calls himself king of the Cephallenians, and some verses later [[XXIV, 5, 429], Antinous' father complains that Odysseus killed the bravest of the Cephallenians. The name of the island of Cephallenia is, however, absent from Homer, the four islands of which the dominion of Odysseus is composed being called Ithaca, Dulichion, Same, and Zacynthus [*this island's modern Greek name is Zakinthos*]. ... the people of the Kephallenes, as the Greek form is, have given their name to the island of Cephallenia, which in the Homeric age was called by another name, be it Dulichion, as Professor Dörpfeld and his followers think, be it Same as the old opinion is. ... The name of the island of Cephallenia appears for the first time in Herodotus [5th century BC].' [10]

Sami is the port on Cephallonia from which today you take the ferry to Ithaca, and so it seems only sensible to assume that the name of the town is a survival of the original name of the island, and that Cephallonia was in ancient times called Samē. Sami is the main point of communication today by boat between Ithaca and Cephallonia, as it probably was in antiquity as well. In that sense it was the focal point of the ancient island, so that it could have retained the name alone, which at one time had been loosely applied to the entire island. We have a parallel to this with Lesbos, which in both ancient and modern times has often been called simply 'Mytilene' after its main port, even though everyone knows perfectly well that that is only a kind of shorthand and is not really accurate. As for Dulichion, it must have been the ancient name of Leucas. In the *Odyssey*, Zakinthos is described as 'wooded', Ithaca is described as 'stony', and Dulichion is described as 'the grain-growing island', and the main attraction to trading vessels.

It is also made clear in the epic that Ithaca was small, since the numbers of suitors to Penelope from each of the four islands are given as follows in Book XVI: 52 suitors from Dulichion together with 6 armourers, 24 from Samē, 20 from Zakinthos, and only 12 from Ithaca. How can Ithaca possibly have been the enormous island of Cephallonia and only have produced 12 suitors, the smallest number of all? This is clear proof from within the epic itself that ancient Ithaca cannot have been modern Cephallonia.

As anyone who has been to those beautiful islands knows very well, Cephallonia is much larger than Ithaca, but Ithaca has a marvellous charm, so that many people prefer it. If one were king of the four islands: Leucas, Ithaca, Cephallonia, and Zacynthus, as they are known today, one would choose Ithaca as the site of one's palace. The site which we investigated offered unique advantages over any other spot in the four islands. First of all, in a distant age when landscape features were crucial, it was situated in the prominent and dramatic 'V' formation shown so clearly in Plates 10 and 11.

Plate 8. The V-formation as seen from the site of the Palace, looking out to sea. From the site of the Palace of Odysseus, you can see three seas. But the most striking sea view of all is this one, looking across at the Island of Cephallonia (or Kephalonia). We see that the island is framed in a giant 'V' formed by the hills on either side. I believe that this was the striking landscape feature which Odysseus himself would have seen (in reverse) when sailing to and from his home on Ithaca (This was not the case upon his return from Troy, because he was asleep then.). Apart from a few modern buildings barely visible in the far distance, and of course far fewer trees existing than in his day, this is precisely the key scene which Odysseus saw from his own sailing ship to tell him he was nearly home. As seen from the sea, the Palace of Odysseus can readily be located as situated in the hills behind this prominent 'V' formation of the landscape of Ithaca. Such a palace location may partially have been chosen for ease of identification by a seafaring people at a time when there were few landmarks other than natural landscape features. In sailing round his island, 'V marked the spot' where the home of Odysseus could be found. (*Photo by Robert Temple*)

Plate 9. The V-formation, looking inland. This view of the 'V'-formation of the intersecting hillsides of Ithaca, giving the location of the Palace of Odysseus, is taken from a hill beside the sea looking inland. It resembles the view which can be seen from a boat, except that it is higher and less striking. (*Photo by Robert Temple*)

This giant 'V' in the landscape, indicating the site of the palace to seafarers, can be seen as a prominent indicator from ships. Then, the three separate harbours all opening to different bays (the three 'seas' of ancient tradition) of the north of the island can all be conveniently monitored from the site of the palace. The modern Greek names of these are Ormos Friko and Ormos Afales (the Harbours of Frikes and Afales), and Steno Ithakis (the Strait of Ithaca), with its mini-harbour at Polis, and its sea cave Louizou, later sacred to Odysseus as demi-god.

Plate 10. The Bay of Polis, or *Steno Ithakis* (Strait of Ithaca), as seen from the site of the Palace of Odysseus. Polis has a small harbour and is also the location of the sea-cave of Louizou, which achieved a sacred status in relation to Odysseus as a demi-god. The view is as seen from the site of the palace, looking southwest, with Cephallonia in the distance. Ships arriving from the open sea at all three ancient harbours of the Bay could readily be seen from the palace site, giving at least two hours' advance warning to the palace of any incursions by enemies or by pirates. (*Photo by Olivia Temple*)

Plate 11. A photo of the Bay of Polis at Ithaca taken in the 1920s. Reproduced from Wilhelm Dörpfeld, *Alt-Ithaka* (*Ancient Ithaca*), Munich, 1927, Volume Two, Plate 1 facing p. 442.

From the site, anyone could be seen coming long before they could reach the palace. Advance warning of any arrival would be at least two hours, even if they were armed soldiers inclined to rush up the hill at a full run, having leapt from their ships as invaders or pirates. (In antiquity pirates were a constant and serious scourge of the Mediterranean.) The palace was thus safe from any possibility of surprise attack by sea. No surprise attack was possible from the south by land because of the difficulty of the terrain and the inevitability of local warning. So therefore the palace site was uniquely secure as a location and could be recognised from a boat at sea by the initiated by means of a dramatic and unmistakeable sign in the natural landscape. It therefore makes perfect and unrivalled sense in the kingdom of the four islands as the location for the royal palace.

Heurtley found a great deal of evidence of Mycenaean occupation at our site. However, his finds made clear that this site had been occupied since Minoan times, and it was not merely Mycenaean. On the other hand, occupation of the palace site seems to cease abruptly at the end of the Mycenaean age, known as 'Late Helladic III' [ending approximately 1200 BC], indicating that the palace ceased to be inhabited after the collapse of Mycenaean civilisation, and was never a site of habitation again. Heurtley summarises as follows:

' ... we have at Pelicata,

1. A site naturally adapted for a Mycenaean citadel, and one selected by many scholars, on topographical grounds, as the site of the palace of Odysseus.

2. Evidence of an extensive pre-Mycenaean settlement, which there is reason for thinking was continuously occupied until and during L H III [Late Helladic III] times.

3. Late Helladic III sherds, belonging to the phase that preceded the traditional date of the Trojan war, and none later.

4. Traces of buildings of good masonry on the summit and of a circuit-wall just below it, neither of which seem to be later than that period and both of which may belong to it.

'The cumulative value of all this evidence is respectable, and if we add that of Mycenaean sherds (also 13th century [BC]), found by us at Stavros [*the town immediately south of Pelicata*], and at the fountain of Asprosykia, a short distance from it, and if we add that of the ex-voto plaque, bearing the inscription "a vow to Odysseus", found in the cave-sanctuary at Polis [*a small harbour town just beyond Stavros with the sea cave of Louizou which contained a shrine to Odysseus*], which show that the place was associated with Odysseus several centuries after his death, it is clear that those who hold, on other grounds, that the hill of Pelicata was in Homer's mind, when he described the palace of Odysseus, the city and its fountain, may now support their view by a certain amount of archaeological evidence.'[11]

The evidence for worship of Odysseus as a demi-god or 'hero' shown by the plaque found in the sea cave is connected with the widespread worship of many of the Homeric heroes in this way throughout the Mediterranean, and there is little doubt that the Ithacan centre of the worship of Odysseus was the site below the small cliff on the hilltop of Pelicata (Plate 3), where an apparent hill shrine to Odysseus, known as an Odysseion, was appropriately situated at the very foot of what had once been the hero's own home. Aristotle is but one of the ancient writers who refers to the worship of Homeric heroes. In his *Rhetoric* he refers in passing, in the context of discussing examples of common facts, to the worship of Achilles and other Homeric heroes as demi-gods in his own time:

'By common I mean, for instance, praising Achilles because he is a man, or one of the demigods, or because he went on the expedition against Troy; for this is applicable to many others as well, so that such praise is no more suited to Achilles than to Diomedes.'
[12]

To Aristotle and people of his time, the worship of the Homeric heroes was so common and widespread amongst the common folk that it called for no special comment at all, and could merely be mentioned casually like this, as one of the things which one took for granted. In fact, there were shrines to Achilles, Odysseus, and the others in countless places throughout greater Greece, which included southern Italy, which was settled by Greeks. Odysseus had special associations with southern Italy, and many of his fantasy episodes are closely associated with that locale. In fact, his visit to the Underworld was actually located at the Oracle of the Dead at Baia, of which a lengthy description with photos has been published by myself in my book entitled *Netherworld (Oracles of the Dead* in the American edition).[13] Subsequent to the publication of that book, I returned with a film crew and made a documentary film about the Baian Oracle of the Dead entitled in Britain *Descent into Hell* (Channel Four, 2004), and in the USA entitled *Voices from Hell* (National Geographic Channel, 2004). Baia itself was named after Baios, a companion of Odysseus who is not mentioned in the *Odyssey*, but whose name is preserved in the many further Odysseus legends which survived in other ancient sources, such as the lost plays about Odysseus by the Athenian dramatists, and the South Italian histories by ancient historians such as Timaeus of Locri. There is a huge field of enquiry here, and an entire book could be written about the history of the Odysseus legends and their geographical and topographical associations, and very many accounts have already been published on different aspects of this subject. The Sirens were said to be located south of Baia near Sorrento. Circe lived north of Baia, also on the coast of Italy. The Clashing Rocks were said to be at the Straits of Messina. The topography of the fantasy Odysseus seems to have been Italian, but the topography of the 'Return' was wholly Ithacan, - surely this is further evidence that these two elements of the *Odyssey* were not originally joined and came from two different geographical regions, before being fused together.

As if all these issues were not perplexing enough, there is the possibility that the *Iliad* and the *Odyssey* were not written by the same poet. In 1955, Denys Page published a rather notorious book entitled *The Homeric Odyssey*, in which he made such embarrassing comments as these:

'Consider finally that the *Odyssey*, although it presupposes the story of the siege of Troy, *"never repeats or refers to any incident related in the Iliad"* (Munro, *Od.*, ii, 325). It is as if the Odyssean poet were wholly ignorant of that particular story which is told in the *Iliad*. Nowhere is there any allusion to the wrath of Achilles or to the death of Hector, or indeed to any other incident, large or small, described in the *Iliad*. … the *Odyssey* shows no awareness of the existence of the *Iliad*, is generally thought (by the few who notice it) to afford a problem, for which no very pleasing solution is suggested: to me it affords no problem, but only comfort and corroboration – the reason why the *Iliad* is ignored by the Odyssean poet is simply that the *Iliad* was unknown to him.' [14]

Many of the aspects of the siege of Troy which are familiar parts of the general story are not mentioned at all in the *Iliad*. For instance, the Trojan Horse is not mentioned even once, the 'Achilles heel' is not mentioned, the judgement of Paris is not mentioned overtly but only hinted at once in the final book in an indirect manner, and the name of Iphigeneia is nowhere mentioned, even though she was the daughter of Agamemnon whom he wished to sacrifice in order to get to Troy. The oaths of the suitors of Helen, sworn to her father Tyndareus, that they would all come to the aid of whichever should become her husband, are not mentioned in the *Iliad*, and the name of Tyndareus is not even mentioned. This is odd, since it is those oaths which bound all the Greeks to go to Troy in the first place, and is why they are said to have followed Menelaus on his madcap expedition. – All these things which most people familiar with the tale of Troy assume are in the *Iliad* are not there at all! They really come from other sources.

The Trojan Horse is mentioned in the *Odyssey* but not in the *Iliad*! In Book VIII of the *Odyssey*,[15] when Odysseus is with the Phaeacians, before returning to Ithaca (and hence this occurs in one of the 'magical sections which I believe to have been intruded into the Epic), the minstrel bard Demodocus is summoned to perform for Odysseus. After a feast, Demodocus plays his lyre and sings his tales. Odysseus asks him to sing of the fate of the Greeks (Achaeans) and their struggles at Troy as if he, Demodocus, had been present or had heard it from another person. He then specifically asks Demodocus to sing of 'the building of the horse of wood' which he himself (Odysseus) had taken up to the Trojan citadel as a trick, having filled it with men who then sacked Troy. He challenges him to get the details right and says that if Demodocus can do this, he will praise him to all mankind as having the gift of divine song. Demodocus then sings the tale and tells the details. Odysseus is so moved he bursts into tears.

Nowhere in the *Odyssey* is there any mention of the original home of the bard Demodocus, and yet he is described as Demodocus of Corcyra (modern Corfu) in the treatise *On Music* which has sometimes been ascribed to Plutarch, but was apparently the work of another author whose identity is not known. The author, who is now called by classical scholars 'Pseudo-Plutarch' because he is not really Plutarch, though in fairness he never claimed to be (the attribution to Plutarch was made centuries later, the author's real name having not survived in the manuscript), says of him (in the Loeb translation):

'There was also an ancient musician, Demodocus of Corcyra, who composed a *Sack of Troy* and a *Marriage of Aphrodite and Hephaestus* …'[16]

The earlier translation by Bromby reads:

'In this list of the early musicians are included Demodocus of Corcyra, who wrote *The Fall of Troy*, and *The Marriage of Venus and Vulcan* …'[17]

In the treatise it is explained that this information is taken from Heraclides of Ponticus (a contemporary of Plato) 'in his collection of notices respecting Music' (Bromby's translation; Loeb merely says 'in his *Collection*', leaving out the specific statement that it was a *Synagōgē* specifically concerning music). The historian of ancient music, Andrew Barker, is not certain of the exact title of this work, but thinks it was either *Collection of Musicians* or *Collection of Facts about Music*.[18] I think both of those are rather ungainly, but that the latter is closer to the truth. The work of Heraclides is lost, but this fragment is now known as the Heraclides Fragment 157 as edited by F. Wehrli. It was thus clearly Heraclides who reported the fact unmentioned in the *Odyssey* that Demodocus was from Corcyra. The point of my mentioning this is to show that Heraclides and Pseudo-Plutarch had more information about Demodocus than was available from the *Odyssey*, and hence the suggestion that he composed a work concerning *The Sack of Troy* is not just an assumption based upon the passage in the *Odyssey*.

The epics were probably not extant in written form until the sixth century BC, and before that they were preserved in oral tradition. No exact written text existed within a reasonable time of the life of Homer or of the other epic poets of his time. Many minor variants in the texts of Homer are known today, preserved in quotations made in ancient times. It is interesting that it was in his youth that Aristotle seems to have been so disturbed by discrepancies in the Homeric texts that, according to two of his biographers, he actually attempted to prepare a standard edition of the *Iliad*,[19] which is the version of the epic which he gave to Alexander, as described earlier. Aristotle also wrote an extensive book, *Homeric Questions*, which was mentioned earlier, which is lost except for a few fragments (Rose, Fragments 142-179, which have apparently never been translated by anyone into any modern language). Aristotle's visit to Ithaca and his research for the *Constitution of the Ithacans* (a lost work) must have contributed considerably to this other work, concerned as he was with the subject of the ancient kingdom of Odysseus, and we see in the account at the end of this book that he found a different version of the *Odyssey* in existence in Ithaca than in Athens! In the fourth century BC, therefore, serious scholars were already rather desperate about discrepancies and variations in the Homeric texts. Such issues, related as they are to the major issues of integrity of authorship and integrity of texts of both the *Iliad* and the *Odyssey*, are of direct relevance to the reliability of details concerning Ithaca, the historical Odysseus, and his palace. But having called attention to these matters at some length because of their importance, we cannot resolve them here, and so we turn to the topographical evidence to be found in the *Odyssey*.

Odysseus finally returns home to Ithaca in Book XIII of the *Odyssey*. It is a strange homecoming, for he has been rowed there by the Phaeacians, and when they arrive at Ithaca, Odysseus is asleep. They lift him up, carry him from the boat, and leave him asleep on the shore! They stack his goods and his presents beside him, and then they just sail away. This episode is so extraordinarily strange that I marvel that it is rarely if ever discussed. Perhaps it is meant to represent a trance or shaman-like state of the hero, who returns home from a dream-voyage, having never really been away at all. I find this episode stranger than the more famous magical episodes with monsters and enchantresses.

Side by side with this strange aspect, however, is the extraordinarily mundane description of the small Ithacan harbour, as if written by a local. The juxtaposition of the bizarre and the banal in this section of the *Odyssey* is jarring in the extreme. The point at which Odysseus awakens from his shaman-like sleep is apparently the point at which the original epic, let us call it the *Return of Odysseus*, began. From that point on, things become very ordinary, and the magical events cease. However, the detailed description of the small harbour or cove is incorporated just before this. There is a careful description of the cove as containing a revered sea cave sacred to the nymphs, or Naiads (as the sea nymphs were called). This may be intended as a description of the small Harbour of Polis, where the sea cave (which alas can no longer be entered safely) yielded upon excavation many decades ago a votive tablet to the demi-god Odysseus, as mentioned earlier. This is the cave in which Odysseus hides his things after awaking, before setting out to reclaim his palace. And Odysseus, upon his return to Ithaca, is recognised only by his faithful old dog, Argos, who greets him because he recognises his scent.

Plates 12 and 13. The front and back of a silver denarius coin minted at Rome in 82 BC. The front shows the head of the god Hermes (called Mercury by the Romans), with his winged cap to show that he is the messenger of the gods. And on the reverse we see Odysseus returning to Ithaca, with his walking stick and traveller's cap, being greeted by his dog, who recognises him. This is an idealised scene, for in the *Odyssey* Homer says: "There lay the hound Argos, full of vermin; yet even now, when he marked Odysseus standing near, he wagged his tail and dropped both his ears, but nearer to his master he had no longer strength to move." And at that very moment of recognition of his returned master, the poor old dog died, having lived long enough to see his master one last time.

Figure 5. A depiction from an ancient gem of Odysseus being recognised by his old hound, Argos (Argus), upon his return to his home on the Island of Ithaca, after his long wanderings. Argos, who remembers his scent, knows him, but no one else recognises him after such a long time away. Argos seems to be depicted emerging from a dog flap at the base of one of the towers at a corner of the forecourt of the Palace. Soon after greeting his old master, Argos dies. Reproduced from Wilhelm H. Roscher, *Ausführliches Lexikon der Griechischen und Römischen Mythologie* (*Copious Lexicon of Greek and Roman Mythology*), Leipzig, 1897-1902, Vol. 3, Part 1, p. 674. Roscher copied it from a previous publication by Johannes Overbeck. (*Collection of Robert Temple*)

But what of the two cliffs on either side of the harbour sloping to the sea which the epic specifically mentions as the defining feature of this harbour? I believe they are precisely the gigantic 'V' formation to be seen in Plates 10 and 11, which is a natural landscape feature formed by two sloping cliffs making a dramatic sign which can be seen from the sea to indicate the location of the palace on a hilltop in the centre of the 'V'. The fact that the *Odyssey* apparently mentions this landscape feature shows the extent of the local topographical knowledge embodied in this section of the epic, and of course goes a long way towards validating the identity of the ancient Ithaca and the modern Ithaca.

Various features of Ithaca are mentioned in the end of Book XIII of the epic, a mountain covered with a forest named either Neion or Neriton, a rock called Raven's Rock, and a well of Arethousa, but of course we cannot be certain of the names of these places today. Some Greek scholar with meticulously detailed knowledge of the topography of Ithaca might have views on these matters, but I have none. At the beginning of Book XIV, Odysseus 'went up from the cove through wooded ground, taking a stony trail into the high hills …'[20] This is all very appropriate, as may be seen from Plate 14, which is a typical ancient stony track leading from the site of the Palace of Odysseus down to the sea. But he stops short and does not climb all the way to the palace, and he visits his old swine-herd, Eumaios.

Plate 14. This charming and heavily-scented pathway lined with high myrtle hedges winds its way from the hilltop where the Palace of Odysseus once stood all the way down to the sea. Possibly it follows a path which has been used by the local inhabitants for millennia. (*Photo by Robert Temple*)

The descriptions of the Palace of Odysseus commence in Book XVI, where the suitors are described before Odysseus arrives amongst them. The first point which is clear is that the arrivals of ships can be seen from there. The suitor Amphinomos at one point easily peers out over the bay from the hilltop and spots the arrival of the ship of Telemachus[21]. This is very much in accord with our site, as I have already described, from which all three harbours can be seen.

When the suitors leave the palace to go outside for a meeting, we are told:

'Out of the house, out of the court they went, beyond the wall and gate, to sit in council.'[22]

This is a very accurate description of a Mycenaean palace. They had been sitting in the great hall, called the *megaron*, and rose and passed out into the open but enclosed courtyard known as the *aulē*, and through the porch and presumably even outside the circuit wall of the precinct. This means that they went southwards from the palace. All Mycenaean palaces were constructed like this, and all opened to the south for reasons of sun.

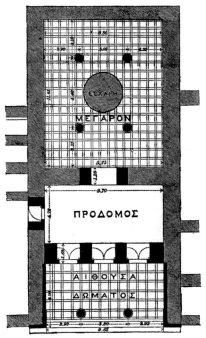

Plan of Men's Apartment.

Figure 6. This plan shows details of the palace at Tiryns, near Argos, dating from the time of Odysseus. At top is the Great Hall known as the *Megaron*, and the large circle in the middle represents the giant hearth which heated the room and served also as the centre for cooking. Reproduced from Charles Diehl, *Excursions in Greece*, London, 1893, p. 54.

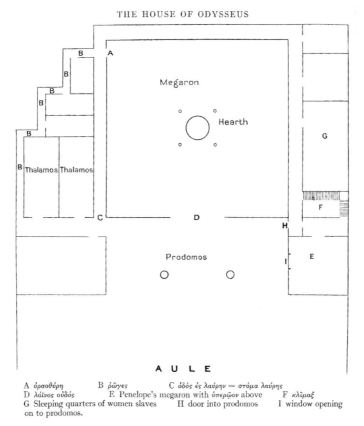

A ὀρσοθύρη   B ῥῶγες   C ὁδὸς ἐς λαύρην = στόμα λαύρης
D λάϊνος οὐδός   E Penelope's megaron with ὑπερῷον above   F κλῖμαξ
G Sleeping quarters of women slaves   H door into prodomos   I window opening
on to prodomos.

Figure 7. A plan drawing which appears in H. L. Lorimer's study of Homeric subjects, which is intended to show the layout of the Palace of Odysseus as described in Homer, according to Lorimer's interpretation. At the bottom is the open Courtyard (the *aulē*), and at the top is the roofed *Megaron*, which was the Great Hall used by the men, at the centre of which was the huge open hearth which provided the heat for the hall and the place for cooking. (The smoke went up and made its way out through the roof, under the eaves of a raised portion.) Lorimer has designated what he believes to have been Penelope's private apartments (on an upper floor) by the letter E. He believes the household slaves, of which there would have been many, slept in a communal room marked with the letter G. Reproduced from H. L. Lorimer, *Homer and the Monuments*, Macmillan, London, 1950, p. 408, Fig. 59.

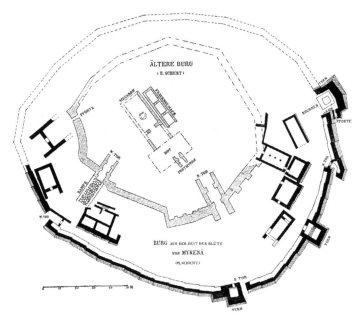

Figure 8. A plan of the ancient city of Troy of the Mycenaean era, at the time of the Trojan War. The central structure, which is rectangular in shape and shown at an angle, is the Palace of King Priam, where Paris and Helen also lived. The German word 'Hof' means 'court', and is the courtyard of the Palace, which had no roof. The long rectangular room at the back is the *Megaron*, and the circular shape in the centre represents the central hearth fire of the hall. The women's quarters ("Frauengemach') are off to the right of the *Megaron* in this instance. (Reproduced from H. Luckenbach, *Kunst und Geschichte (Art and History)*, Munich and Berlin, 1910, p. 19, Figure 30.)

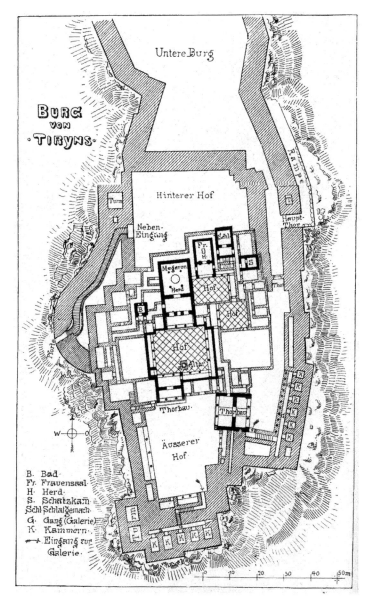

Figure 9. Plan of the Palace of Tiryns near Argos, of the time of Odysseus. Near the centre of the plan, with a circle in the centre depicting the giant hearth, is the *Megaron*, the Great Hall of the Palace. The *Hof* is the Courtyard, which had no roof. This palace was larger and more elaborate than that of Odysseus. Reproduced from H. Luckenbach, *Kunst und Geschichte (Art and History)*, Part One, Munich and Berlin, 1910, p. 20, Figure 32.

Figure 10. A reconstruction of the appearance of the Palace of Tiryns near Argos, which dated from the time of Odysseus. The central hall with the three pillars in front was the *Megaron*, or Great Hall. (In fact, the reconstruction should more accurately have shown a raised portion of the roof in the centre, to allow the smoke to escape from the central hearth below.) Just before the *Megaron* is the open Courtyard. And in front of that is an 'Outer Courtyard', though Odysseus's Palace, being a provincial king's palace rather than a metropolitan one, would only have had the single Courtyard. The plan of this palace may be seen in Figure 9. Reproduced from H. Luckenbach, *Kunst und Geschichte (Art and History)*, Part One, Munich and Berlin, 1910, p. 21, Figure 35.

Figure 11. The Palace of Odysseus at Ithaca would have had a plan similar to this one, or perhaps even identical, and if excavations are carried out, this is what the foundations will look like. The door opening at the bottom of the plan opens to the south. In the centre of the plan is the large hall known as the *Megaron*, where the men gathered. The two rows of columns in that hall tended to be of wood set on stone bases, holding aloft an inner wooden roof which was slightly raised above the main roof, and which was open to the air along its base, to allow the smoke from the central heath in the hall to escape, and to let light in. The small shaded circle in the *Megaron* represents the central hearth fire. The women's hall in this plan is directly behind (in this case, shown above) the *Megaron*. The bottom square portion of the plan is the open forecourt of the Palace. The tiny square shape in the centre of it is the Altar to Zeus which is mentioned as being at that very location in the *Odyssey*. (Reproduced from Bertha Carr Rider, *The Greek House*, Cambridge, 1965, Figure 34 on p. 173).

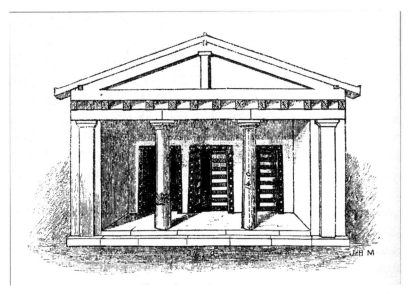

Figure 12. This is what the front of the *Megaron* of the Palace of Odysseus would have looked like, as seen from the unroofed courtyard in front of it. The space behind the columns, but in front of the doors leading into the hall, was the Porch. It was in the Porch that visitors were accommodated overnight, on portable beds which were set up for them by the servants and slaves, who also supplied piles of rugs and animal skins if the weather was cold, as well as portable fires. But in the good weather, it was pleasant to sleep here, and to look up at the stars and breathe in the fresh night air. Aromatic herbs would have been burnt all night in charcoal braziers to keep away the mosquitoes. (Reproduced from Bertha Carr Rider, *The Greek House*, Cambridge, 1965, Figure 22, p. 130, where it is reproduced from an earlier work by Wilhelm Dörpfeld.)

At the end of Book Sixteen, there is a mention of Hermes's Ridge above the town of one of the harbours, but this too can presumably not be readily identified today. (I do not have enough familiarity with the local or folk place names to be aware whether any of these names given in the *Odyssey* may survive in any form today.) The town was always separate from the palace in Mycenaean times. The palace was a self-contained entity which had an outer circuit wall of the precinct and inside that its own palace wall and palisade as well. Therefore, the description of a ridge being above the town does not mean that there was a ridge above the palace. The Hermes Ridge referred to is a ridge above a harbour, and the palace overlooked three harbours from its hilltop.

In Book XVII, the suitors are described as 'swaggering before Odysseus' hall, … competing at the discus-throw and javelin, on the level measured field.'[23] The hilltop of our site is extensive, and there is plenty of level ground there for such a place to have existed. After the suitors go back into the great hall to dine, the disguised Odysseus and the swine-herd 'were on their way out of the hills to town'.[24] This is a very good description of the topography, for to get to any town, one did indeed have to make one's way 'out of the hills'. On their way 'down to the city', Odysseus and the swineherd pass a spring which is named Clearwater:

'Down by the stony trail they made their way as far as Clearwater, not far from town – a spring house where the people filled their jars. … round it on the humid ground (was) a grove, a circular wood of poplars …'[25]

Perhaps this was the spring mentioned by Heurtley, which today is called Asprosykia, at Stavros, and literally 'not far from the town', if we consider Stavros, the modern town nearest to Pelicata, as the ancient town referred to here. For in the *Odyssey* a local town and a harbour city seem both to be referred to, as separate places.

The number of named features in the ancient Ithacan landscape strongly suggests an intimate familiarity with the island on the part of the author of this section of the *Odyssey*. When the disguised Odysseus returns up to the hill again to the palace, we have this description:

'Reaching the gate, Odysseus and the forester halted and stood outside, for harp notes came around them rippling on the air as Phemios picked out a song. Odysseus caught his companion's arm and said: "My friend, here is the beautiful place – who could mistake it? Here is Odysseus' hall: no hall like this! See how one chamber grows out of another; see how the court is tight with wall and coping; no man-at-arms could break this gateway down!'[26]

It is interesting that the terms in which the palace is praised stress its security against armed attack, for its very situation was chosen for that reason, as I have previously explained. Then Odysseus enters the great hall, or *megaron*, disguised as a mendicant 'humped like a bundle of rags over his stick' and:

'He settled on the inner ash-wood sill, leaning against the door jamb – cypress timber the skilled carpenter planed years ago and set up with a plumb-line.'[27]

The same doorway is described again in Book XVIII:

'Under the lofty doorway, on the door-sill of wide smooth ash, they held this rough exchange.'[28]

This is a typical inner doorway to a Mycenaean great hall, which sometimes, though not in the *Odyssey*, featured a double-door (two doors separated by a vestibule) leading out into the walled courtyard. One key feature of such structures is that there was only this one way in or out of the great hall, which becomes crucial to the story later on. While Odysseus is in the great hall, begging scraps from the suitors, he is savagely struck by one of them, and the poet says: 'Penelope on the higher level of her room had heard the blow, and knew who gave it.'[29] This indicates that Penelope's living quarters were on the upper storey, reached by an inner chamber at the back of the great hall, and so connected with it that sound travelled. This was typical of the Mycenaean palaces. Moments later, Penelope laughs in her chamber when she hears her son let out a 'thundering sneeze' within the great hall below. The intimacy with which Mycenaean lords and ladies of great halls had to live with their retainers was such that little could escape anyone's notice. Everything was centred round the great open hearth of the hall, the smoke of which went out through a hole in the roof. There were chairs and benches covered with fleeces[30] ranged around the walls of the hall, and stools filling the open space, where all and sundry were welcome and feasted together. Very substantial numbers of people could congregate in these huge halls, and the presence of a hundred feasting people was not unusual. Fresh beasts were slaughtered for meat on a daily basis, as the *Odyssey* specifically states. The reason why there was only one door in and out of the great hall was because of the central hearth, as a door opening at the back of the hall would have resulted in intolerable smoke and draughts. Towards the back of the hall, various chambers opened for the private use of the lord's family, and these were often of two storeys. The women spent most of the day sitting at the back of the great hall spinning wool and gossiping, and they retired to the most remote of the private chambers at night, which they locked behind them. They are described again in Book XVIII, when Penelope descends the stairs from her chambers to the great hall: 'She rose and left her glowing upper room, and down the stairs, with her two maids in train ...'[31] There was a strong respect, amounting almost to a taboo, shown by outsiders towards entering the inner chambers leading from the back of the great hall in a Mycenaean palace. This is referred to by Penelope herself in the epic, when she complains that the beggar who says he has news of Odysseus (who is really the disguised Odysseus himself) will not let himself be led into her chambers to tell her his tales directly:

'Have you not brought him? Why? What is he thinking? Has he some fear of overstepping? Shy about these inner rooms?'[32]

Early in Book XIX, when a confrontation with the suitors is nearing, Telemachos takes the precautions of securing the women's quarters:

'He called Eurykelia, the nurse, and told her: "Nurse, go shut the women in their quarters while I shift Father's armour back to the inner rooms ... I want them shielded from the draught and smoke. ..." ... Straight back she went to lock the doors of the women's hall.'[33]

The 'women's hall', or women's *megaron*, was a smaller hall of their own to which they could retreat when they wished to leave the rear of the main great hall, where they tended to sit north of the central hearth if they wished to be present but discreetly separated when males were present. It was behind this private women's hall that the women's actual chambers lay.

Since structures of this type ceased with the decline of Mycenaean civilisation, the poet's comprehension of architectural dynamics and layout as it effects the story is certainly impressive, and indicates a strong verbal tradition going back to the time when palaces of this kind still existed, which by the much later time of Homer they did not. It is really as if Homer himself had lived in one of these palaces, so intimate was his familiarity with the details of their construction, as shown again in Book XVIII:

'Then, by the ankle-bone, Odysseus hauled the fallen one outside, crossing the courtyard to the gate, and piled him against the wall.'[34]

This is a very precise description of the layout, a man being dragged from the great hall out into the courtyard, across it to the front gate. But since such great halls and courtyards and front gates no longer existed in Homer's time, how did he have this close feel for the minutiae of the action? The answer may lie in a very exact preservation of earlier verbal accounts, which Homer retained unaltered. And if that be the case, then the topographical and architectural features described must be just as minutely preserved, and every bit as important. However, there is one alternative possibility as to how Homer came to know the details of this long-abandoned palace so intimately, despite many centuries having elapsed. I shall give that explanation a little later.

Sons of great families often had their own separate chambers off the courtyard rather than off the great hall, as was the case with Telemachos, the son of Odysseus, who 'went across the hall and out under the light of torches – crossed the court to the tower chamber where he had always slept.'[35] Such towers, generally of wood, either stood in the centre of the courtyard, or were part of the courtyard walls. They are one of the least understood aspects of Mycenaean palaces, due to the fact that their remains were perishable and did not tend to survive.

At the beginning of Book XX, Odysseus beds down in the palace porch to sleep.

This too is an accurate account of where visitors to Mycenaean palaces slept. H. L. Lorimer, in his substantial book *Homer and the Monuments*, explains that all visitors at all times in such palaces slept in the porch at the front of the courtyard, whether they were beggars lying on ox skins covered by fleeces, or dignitaries to whom proper beds were given (for instance, Telemachos was given a bed in the porch of the Palace of Menelaus when he visited him):

'... the porch in all cases served as the bedroom of a guest, whatever his rank. The reason is obvious. Hospitality extended to all strangers, with or without credentials, and the porch conceded a roof without giving admission, as the vestibule would have done, to the interior of the house.'[36]

When they were getting ready to slaughter the suitors in the great hall, Telemachos seated his father, still disguised as a beggar, in a key position:

'Telemakhos [Telemachos] placed his father to advantage just at the door-sill of the pillared hall, setting a stool there and a sawed-off table, gave him a share of tripes, poured out his wine in a golden cup ...'[37]

When he reveals his true identity to the swineherd and the cowherd, Odysseus, preparing for the slaughter of the suitors, asks them to do some things to help him:

'Tell the women to lock their own door tight. Tell them if someone hears the shock of arms or groans of men, in hall or court, not one must show her face, but keep still at her weaving. ... run to the outer gate [of the courtyard] and lock it. Throw the cross-bar and lash it.'[38]

After Odysseus reveals himself, he begins to slay the suitors one by one with arrows, and his son kills one with a spear. But finally he runs out of arrows. It is at this point in Book XXII, with Odysseus and Telemachos supported by the armed swineherd and cowherd, who were faithful old retainers of the palace, that some interesting details about the palace layout are revealed:

'While he had arrows he aimed and shot, and every shot brought down one of his huddling enemies. But when all barbs had flown from the bowman's fist, he leaned his bow in the bright entry-way beside the door, and armed: a four-ply shield hard on his shoulder, and a crested helm, horsetailed, nodding stormy upon his head, then took his tough and bronze-shod spears. The suitors who held their feet, no longer under bowshot, could see a window high in a recess of the wall, a vent, lighting the passage to the storeroom. This passage had one entry, with a door, at the edge of the great hall's threshold, just outside. Odysseus told the swine-herd to stand over and guard this door and passage. As he did so, a suitor named Agelaos asked the others: "Who will get a leg up on that window and run to alarm the town? One sharp attack and this fellow will never shoot again." His answer came from the goat-herd foreman Melanthios [*who had turned traitor to Odysseus, unlike the swineherd foreman and the cowherd, or cattle foreman*]: "No chance, my lord. The exit into the courtyard is too near them, too narrow. One good man could hold that portal against a crowd. No: let me scale the wall and bring you arms out of the storage chamber. Odysseus and his son put them indoors, I'm sure of it; not outside."

'The goatish goat-herd clambered up the wall, toes in the chinks, and slipped through to the storeroom. Twelve light shields, twelve spears he took, and twelve thick-crested helms, and handed all down quickly to the suitors. Odysseus, when he saw his adversaries girded and capped and long spears in their hands shaken at him, felt his knees go slack, his heart sink, for the fight was turning grim. He spoke rapidly to his son: "Telemakhos, one of the serving women is tipping the scales against us in this fight, or maybe Melanthios [*the goat-herd*]." But sharp and clear Telemakhos said: "It is my own fault, Father, mine alone. They were more alert than I. Eumaios, go and lock that door …"[39]

Figure 13. This design on a gold ring from Boetia of the Late Helladic Period III, which shows a duel between two spearmen holding tower-shields of the sort used at the time of Odysseus. Sword scabbards hang from their waists. Reproduced from H. L. Lorimer, *Homer and the Monuments*, Macmillan, London, 1950, p. 144, Fig. 7.

Figure 14. At left is another depiction of the typical 'tower shield' of the type used at the time of Odysseus. A design from a gold signet ring found in a Minoan shaft grave. The man on the left is defending himself with a tower shield. The man on the right is wounded or dying. The two men in the centre are fighting with swords in a glen with rocky sides, and according to the Minoan artistic conventions, the rocky background is shown as projecting not only from the bottom and right side of the picture of the battle, but from the top as well (meant to suggest that the men are surrounded by rocks). Reproduced from H. L. Lorimer, *Homer and the Monuments*, Macmillan, London, 1950, Figure 2 on page 140.

Figure 15. An amethyst gem carving from the Late Helladic I period found at Prosymna in the Argolid in Greece. The unfortunate warrior on the left, who is using a Mycenaean tower shield of the time of Odysseus, is being stabbed in the neck. For someone protected by a tower shield, the only accessible places for a mortal wound were either the neck or the head. (Reproduced from H. L. Lorimer, *Homer and the Monuments*, Macmillan, London 1950, p. 142, Figure 5.)

Figure 16. A battle scene at Troy, from an ancient painting. Odysseus is the man holding a shield with a face on its front, second from left. He wears his typical pointed cap, a motif which tended to identify him in Greek art. The men to either side of him are Trojans. Second from right is the mighty warrior Ajax, and at right is a Greek military trumpeter blowing his trumpet to signal the troops. In this scene, the shields in use are not 'tower shields' but the shields of a later era. Reproduced from Wilhelm H. Roscher, *Ausführliches Lexikon der Griechischen und Römischen Mythologie* (*Copious Lexicon of Greek and Roman Mythology*), Leipzig, 1897-1902, Vol. 3, Part 1, p. 659. (*Collection of Robert Temple*)

Figure 17. A small statue of Odysseus preserved in the Vatican Museum. The likeness of the face in profile is identical with that of the Venice statue seen in Plate 15 and in the ancient coin see in Plate 16. There was a remarkable continuity of representation of the face of Odysseus over the centuries, and a great stress was placed upon the need for accuracy in classical times concerning the facial representation. Reproduced from Wilhelm H. Roscher, *Ausführliches Lexikon der Griechischen und Römischen Mythologie* (*Copious Lexicon of Greek and Roman Mythology*), Leipzig, 1897-1902, Vol. 3, Part 1, p. 675. (*Collection of Robert Temple*)

Plate 15. The statue of Odysseus at Venice. Reproduced from Wilhelm H. Roscher, *Ausführliches Lexikon der Griechischen und Römischen Mythologie* (*Copious Lexicon of Greek and Roman Mythology*), Leipzig, 1897-1902, Vol. 3, Part 1, p. 676. (*Collection of Robert Temple*)

Plate 16. An ancient coin minted on the Island of Ithaca shows the profile head of the island's hero Odysseus. This likeness remained fairly constant over many centuries, on coins and on statues, as may been seen for instance in Plates 17 and 18. In this image he is wearing his typical cap. Reproduced from Wilhelm H. Roscher, *Ausführliches Lexikon der Griechischen und Römischen Mythologie* (*Copious Lexicon of Greek and Roman Mythology*), Leipzig, 1897-1902, Vol. 3, Part 1, p. 680. Roscher copied it from a previous publication by Friedrich Imhoof-Blumer, the 19th century numismatist. (*Collection of Robert Temple*)

Figure 18. A head of Odysseus holding a spear and wearing a conical helmet, from an ancient cameo. The facial likeness resembles those of the Ithacan coin and the various statues shown in the Plates. Reproduced from Wilhelm H. Roscher, *Ausführliches Lexikon der Griechischen und Römischen Mythologie* (*Copious Lexicon of Greek and Roman Mythology*), Leipzig, 1897-1902, Vol. 3, Part 1, p. 679. (*Collection of Robert Temple*)

Figure 19. Depiction of Odysseus engraved on an ancient gem. Reproduced from Wilhelm H. Roscher, *Ausführliches Lexikon der Griechischen und Römischen Mythologie* (*Copious Lexicon of Greek and Roman Mythology*), Leipzig, 1897-1902, Vol. 3, Part 1, p. 674. Roscher copied it from a previous publication by Johannes Overbeck. It is described as portraying Odysseus sitting on a cliff at the Island of Ogygia (where he was detained by Calypso for seven years) looking into the distance and wondering if he will ever reach home. (*Collection of Robert Temple*)

We do not need to go into the details of the storeroom. But what is stated clearly here is that the sole door into the great hall from the courtyard was narrow and could easily be held against a crowd by one good man. This is what makes it possible for Odysseus to succeed. At this point, the suitors aim six spears at once at Odysseus in the doorway, and the results are as follows:

'… they all let fly as one man. … One hit the door-post of the hall, another stuck in the door's thick timbering, still others rang on the stone wall, shivering shafts of ash.' Odysseus, his son, and the armed cowherd and swineherd then threw four spears of their own, killing four suitors successfully. The suitors turned and ran backwards in the hall, then re-grouped and threw spears again, and at this point a strange repetition of the text occurs, describing the result of their throws as before, except that this time two small wounds are caused. The slaughter continued and then another interesting detail of the palace emerges, as the minstrel of the suitors, named Phemios, wishes to escape:

'He stood now with his harp, holy and clear, in the wall's recess, under the window, wondering if he should flee that way to the courtyard altar, sanctuary of Zeus, the Enclosure God. Thigh-bones in hundreds had been offered there by Laërtes and Odysseus.'[40]

It was common for an altar to have a prominent place in every Mycenaean palace courtyard, so that the beasts slaughtered for food every day could have their thighs offered to the gods.

Eventually all the suitors were slaughtered, and then attention turned to the many women who had been hanging around as the girlfriends of the suitors:

'Sharply Odysseus said: "These dead must be disposed of first of all. Direct the women. Tables and chairs will be scrubbed with sponges, rinsed and rinsed again. When our great room is fresh and put in order, take them outside, these women, between the roundhouse and the palisade [*the enclosing wall of the courtyard*], and hack them with your sword-blades till you cut the life out of them, and every thought of sweet Aphrodite under the rutting suitors, when they lay down in secret. As he spoke there came the women in a bunch, all wailing, soft tears on their cheeks. They fell to work to lug the corpses out into the courtyard under the gateway [*i.e., the corpses were piled in the porch at the southern outer entrance of the courtyard*], propping one against another as Odysseus ordered, for he himself stood over them. In fear these women bore the cold weight of the dead. The next thing was to scrub off chairs and tables and rinse them down. Telemakhos and the herdsman scraped the packed earth floor with hoes, but made the women carry out all blood and mire. When the great room was cleaned up once again, at swordpoint they forced them out, between the roundhouse and the palisade, pell-mell to huddle in that dead end without exit. Telemakhos, who knew his mind, said curtly: "I would not give the clean death of a beast to trulls who made a mockery of my mother and of me too – you sluts, who lay with suitors."

'He tied one end of a hawser to a pillar and passed the other about the roundhouse top, taking the slack up, so that no one's toes could touch the ground. They would be hung like doves or larks … So now in turn each woman thrust her head into a noose and swung, yanked high in air, to perish there most piteously. Their feet danced for a little, but not long. From storeroom to the court they brought Melanthios [*the traitorous goat-herd*], chopped with swords to cut his nose and ears off, pulled off his genitals to feed the dogs and raging hacked his hands and feet away.'[41]

After all this, the nurse Eurykleia describes what she, Penelope, and the various women of the household (as opposed to the camp follower girls of the suitors) had done during the fight:

'I did not see it, I knew nothing; only I heard the groans of men dying. We sat still in the inner rooms holding our breath, and marvelling, shut in, until Telemakhos came to the door and called me …'[42]

This makes clear that a considerable complex of 'women's quarters' existed behind locked doors at the back of the great hall. Penelope's own chambers were on the upper storey, but the other women evidently had their own chambers beneath hers at ground level.

Another important detail about the palace is revealed in the events which followed. Odysseus was worried about what the locals would think when they learned of the slaughter of the suitors, so to gain time he asked the minstrel to play his harp and his maids to sing, as if a dance and celebration were taking place for the marriage of Penelope to one of the dead suitors:

'... they made the manor hall resound with gaiety of men and grace of women. Anyone passing on the road would say: "Married at last, I see – the queen so many courted. ..." So travellers' thoughts might run – but no one guessed the truth.'[43]

This shows clearly that a main path for local travellers ran very near to the palace palisade, and that passers-by could hear noise inside.

Figure 20. Odysseus sitting and chatting with his wife Penelope at Ithaca immediately after he has killed the suitors and regained possession of his wife and his palace. He is still holding his spear, and has his helmet sitting beside him. Penelope is holding her distaff, a tool used in spinning, which was a Greek woman's traditional task. She has her hand on her husband's knee, as a gesture of affection, and he looks very pleased indeed. She is wearing sandals, with her feet resting on a low stool, and he is barefoot. This image is found on the reverse side of an Etruscan mirror which in 1867 was in the possession of Prince Barberini. Reproduced from Eduard Gerhard, *Etruskische Spiegel* (*Etruscan Mirrors*), Berlin, 1867, Volume IV, Plate CDVI. (*Collection of Robert Temple*)

Thus we come to the end of the important information about the palace, relating to its site and its plan, which can be found in the *Odyssey*.

There are two fundamental books about Mycenaean palaces such as this. The first, by Lorimer, has already been mentioned. But perhaps even more fascinating and informative is Bertha Carr Rider's book *The Greek House*.[44] Bertha Rider's chapter on 'Homeric Palaces' should be read by anyone with a serious interest in this subject.[45]

There is little doubt that if extensive excavations could be carried out on the hilltop at Pelicata, many of the foundations of the Palace of Odysseus could be traced. However, as this was a provincial palace, it did not have a complete stone floor. *The Odyssey* is very explicit about the fact that the great hall had a floor of packed earth, which could be scraped with hoes to remove the blood and gore after the massacre of the suitors. The courtyard would also have had an earth floor, as it was open to the elements. But many of the walls should be traceable. In Plate 6 we see a rock-cut tomb near the site of the palace on the hilltop.

Plate 17. This ancient rock-cut tomb is within the circuit wall boundary of the Palace of Odysseus, on the hilltop very near to where the Palace itself once stood. This photo is taken looking south, and the rectangular depression cut into the top of this outcrop of rock, which we see lengthwise, once contained the body of an important personage associated with this site. The tomb was obviously robbed thousands of years ago. Heurtley believes that the soil level in Mycenaean times was two metres higher on this hilltop, and reached the top of this rock. However, see discussion in the text. (*Photo by Robert Temple*)

Heurtley speculated that this tomb cutting must have been level with the original surface at one time, so that the hilltop must have experienced very drastic soil loss over the past 3200 years. I am sceptical about the reasoning behind this, but it is a suggestion which cannot just be dismissed. Heurtley seems to have been the only person to carry out any excavations at all in the hilltop area, and his ample finds of Mycenaean remains are what we would expect, even though his finds of Minoan remains are somewhat more surprising, and indicate a long tradition for this hilltop extending back centuries before the time of the Trojan War.

We must not forget the extraordinarily vivid descriptions of the palace in the *Odyssey*. The author really does give the impression of having been intimately familiar with the structure and the landscape. The power of the poetic imagination seems to me inadequate to explain this uncanny accuracy. The mysteries of the *Odyssey* deepen in the light of this. It would certainly be of great interest from the point of view of the *Odyssey*, as well as from the point of view of archaeology, to make a thorough investigation of this apparent site of the Palace of Odysseus. I therefore urge a full excavation of the site as early as possible!

I might as well propose one possible explanation for the accuracy of the structural and landscape features in the *Odyssey*. We know from ancient sources that there was a family living in Ithaca many centuries after Mycenaean times who claimed descent from Odysseus. We also have explicit testimony that two hereditary families existed on Ithaca for many centuries called the Koliadai (Colliadi) and the Boukolidai, who claimed to be descended from the two trusty servants of Odysseus mentioned in the *Odyssey*, Eumaois the swine-herd foreman and Philoitis the cow-herd or cattle foreman. They were known to be connected with maintaining the cult and the shrine (see Plate 3) at the foot of the small cliff below the hilltop, which served as both an Odysseion and a Telemachion,[46] where both Odysseus and his son Telemachos were honoured as 'heroes', or demi-gods, for centuries. It is likely that a visit to the shrine would have been combined with a tour of the higher site of the palace itself, where for a fee a so-called 'genuine descendant of Odysseus' (and he might even *really* be genuine, there is no reason why not!) would take you round the foundations of the palace and describe for you in vivid and gory detail the heroic actions which his ancestors had undertaken. One can imagine this easily: 'And here, on this very spot, the great Odysseus stood with his powerful bow, and arrow after arrow flew into the great hall there, as one suitor after another dropped dead. … And over here, this is the porch where the bodies of the suitors were stacked. … Now I will take you through the remains of the great hall and we can enter the women's hall beyond, and then see the remains of the actual chambers of the household.' …

If one realizes that the guides at this place actually claimed direct descent from the swine-herd and the cow-herd of Odysseus, one can more readily understand the somewhat bizarre and inflated importance attached to these individuals in the *Odyssey*. What I think happened was that an epic poet (call him Homer if you wish) visited Ithaca and was shown round by these people claiming descent. He was thrilled with the vivid descriptions of each incident that took place at each spot, as recounted by the enthusiastic guides, who doubtless gave one a full afternoon's entertainment, stressing the importance of their own swine-herd and cow-herd ancestors out of all proportion at the same time. Inspired by this experience, the poet then decided to have a proper look round all the island, and then to compose an epic poem on this wonderful subject, which was bound to be a hit with the people who paid bards to recite their poems. – And it was! And either he or some later poet decided to go further, and tart it up with lots of magical episodes which had no integral connection with the Return of Odysseus, and were not set in Ithaca at all. The result, whether by one poet or by two, was the *Odyssey*. But the version found at Ithaca in the fourth century BC by Aristotle, which has already been mentioned, was by far the more accurate account, which, as Halliday says, 'had its origin in the Ionian islands'.[47]

I think this is how a later poet was able to achieve the amazing intimacy with the locale, the palace, and the island's landscape: he was shown round by guides! And imagination did the rest. Also, having been indoctrinated by the descendants, he duly gave unreasonable prominence to the swine-herd and the cow-herd. (As for the treacherous goat-herd, that may have been a little joke played on the visiting poet by his hosts, who may have been getting their own back in a local feud with another family claiming descent from him!)

Because we know that the site was visited for centuries and was looked after carefully as a family business, and was possibly their main source of income, it is likely that the foundations of the palace were of immense value to the custodians and that for many centuries these people prevented them from being tampered with. It is therefore highly likely that intact foundations should remain below the surface, even though so many stones have subsequently been carried away, as our photo from the 1930s shows so sadly.

There is one other factor which needs to be mentioned. For two and a half thousand years there has been a persistent tradition that Homer was blind. Surely, if he were blind, the hypothesis which I have just given about him being shown round the ruins of the Palace of Odysseus would collapse? I take the opposite view of the matter. There are many peculiarities of the Ithacan section of the *Odyssey* which I find suggestive of the author having been blind, and I am inclined to believe that he was. I suspect that he could see light and darkness, but nothing much else. When you begin to look for traces of this in the epic, you find passages like this in Book XVIII:

'Of mortal creatures, all that breathe or move, earth bears none frailer than mankind. … But when the gods in bliss bring miseries on, then willy-nilly, blindly, he endures. Our minds are as the days are, dark or bright, blown over by the father of gods and men.'[48]

What I find suggestive about this passage is the remark 'Our minds are as the days are, dark or bright …' The poet does not say 'cloudy or fine', 'rainy or sunny', but rather 'dark or bright', which would be what a man suffering from near-blindness, and who can see only to the extent that he can detect the presence or absence of light, would say.

There are two strange references to Penelope's chamber which refer to the amount of light there which could be the comments of a blind man. But most suggestive of all is the bizarre passage where a great white light suddenly appears in the great hall of the palace, in Book XIX:

'… in their path Pallas Athena held up a golden lamp of purest light. Telemakhos at last burst out: "Oh, Father, here is a marvel! All around I see the walls and roof beams, pedestals and pillars, lighted as though by white fire blazing near. One of the gods of heaven is in this place!" Then said Odysseus, the great tactician, "Be still: keep still about it: just remember it. The gods who rule Olympos make this light. You may go off to bed now.'[49]

This strange and unexplained epiphany of divine light suddenly occurs for no reason, and is quickly dismissed. Such an effulgence of a diffuse brightness is the kind of thing a blind man who can only detect the presence or absence of light would experience. Immediately afterwards, as quoted earlier, Telemachos 'went across the hall and out under the light of torches' and crossed the court. This peculiar way of referring to torchlight is also odd. It recognises the presence of torches, beneath which one walks outside in the courtyard, but it does not do so in the way that a sighted person would normally describe them. And not long afterwards Penelope repeatedly asks Odysseus if he thinks her blind, which is another oddity. In fact, the more one scrutinizes the *Odyssey*, the more one finds these niggling details. Of course, if we turn to the magical portions of the epic, we have the famous Polyphemus, the one-eyed Cyclops, and rather detailed descriptions of how he has to feel things rather than see them when his eye has been put out by Odysseus. These passages are very much what a blind man would write, if one were to assume that the same author really did also write the magical sequences.

Figure 21. A sixteenth century woodcut depicting Odysseus putting out the eye of Polyphemus, the one-eyed Cyclops.

And finally, we come to one of the most famous and puzzling phrases in all of ancient literature, the repeated description in the *Odyssey* of 'the wine-dark sea'. Over the years I have read numerous articles in journals by learned scholars trying to explain this phrase, discussing possible perceptions of colour by the ancient Greeks, the meanings and etymologies of words, what Greek wine was like, and all sorts of things which somehow seem rather beside the point and unconvincing. But what I have never seen anyone suggest as an explanation for Homer's famous phrase is this: *Homer may have described the sea as being 'wine-dark' because he had never seen it.*

Let us look at the situation like this: a little boy who is blind grows up on an island and asks his father one day about the sea. 'Can you see fishes swimming in the sea, Father, in the same way you say that you can see birds flying in the air?' 'No, son, that is not possible.' 'Why not, Father?' 'Because the sea is too dark, and you cannot see through it in the way you can see through the air.' 'But I thought the sea was made out of water, Father, and you have often told me that you can see the moss at the bottom of the spring, and the weeds rippling at the bottom of the river. And once you said when you were drinking a cup of water that you could see a pebble at the bottom of your cup. So surely water is not dark?' 'Well, son, water in a cup is not dark, and you can see through it. But the sea is more like wine in a cup, you just can't see to the bottom of it unless you are near the shore.' 'So the sea is dark, then, like wine?' 'Yes, I suppose you could say that it is. The sea is wine-dark, which is why you can rarely see the fishes swimming in it.'

If we now turn our attention back to the site of the palace, imagine a blind poet being led round by the arm and listening intently to the speeches of the guides. Of course he knows when he is 'in the great hall' there is no ceiling left, and that he still feels the breezes and the sun, and he has been told that the walls are not all intact. But nevertheless, as his imagination is fired by the account of the heroic deeds, the great struggle against all odds, and the acts of bravery, and as he relives all of these things in

50

spot after spot, conjuring the action up in his mind, the constructions of his imagination are not contradicted by the evidence of his senses. He does not see with his eyes that the pathetic ruins around which he is being led are only knee-high, and merely traces of a grandeur destroyed centuries ago. To him, the edifice is nearly all still there, his mind's eye sees the walls standing, and there are no physical eyes to tell him otherwise. The vividness with which a blind man can experience a vanished structure is greater than what is possible for any sighted person, as long as he is given powerful descriptions to evoke the full scene. And when he calls it up to memory later, he does not see the ruins covered in weeds, and the tumbledown walls, with stones littering the surface. Instead, he sees the intact palace. He *lives* the vanished picture which only he can see through his imagination because his idea of it is not cluttered or compromised by a knowledge of the present appearance of the ruins. For him, the walls do not stop at the height of the knee, which would be the evidence of the eyes, but they rise all the way to roof height, which is the work of his mind. He has walked and paced the spaces, he has counted the distances, he has by kinaesthetic and tactile means explored the space, and to him it can only be a mental construct. To a blind man, the palace whose spaces he has paced can never be a ruin, for its entirety is implied by the experience of his feet. To this extent, the world inhabited by the blind man is an ideal world, in which all structures which he experiences are complete, and since no imperfections or incompleteness can be seen, they do not exist for him. And this, I believe, is the possible answer to the extreme intimacy which the poet shows with a palace which I believe he went around by foot but which *he could not see was only a ruin.*

I myself have experienced something strangely akin to this. I have been taken round the excavated site of Aristotle's Lyceum in Athens by the woman archaeologist who excavated it. Nothing was more than knee-high, and yet I have been in Aristotle's library, I have been in his lecture room, I have been in the storerooms where he kept his zoological specimens. I know how many steps it is from one to the other, I know how much room there is to turn around in, where the book rolls were kept, where the light vents must have been, where the spring was. I know how far the garden extended down to the river. Although I had eyes to see, and was not being led by the arm, I believe I was really very like the blind Homer being led through the Palace of Odysseus, who marked step by step the size of the courtyard, who knew where the one door to the great hall was, and just how far the arrows would have had to fly and the spears be thrown, and doubtless he walked up the few remaining steps to what he was told had once been Penelope's chambers, so that when he came to write his poem he was constantly referring to these stairs. Every detail was imprinted on his blind man's kinaesthetic memory, he could take you through the place step by step, and in his great poem *he actually did.*

Who knows, perhaps one day we may all be able to walk once more round the site of the palace as people did in the old days when the local family custodians were still there, and ourselves stand beside the stones marking the site of the doorway of the great hall (albeit its sill was of ash and will have perished thousands of year ago), and say to ourselves: 'Here valiant Odysseus stood, with his great bow, and slayed the suitors. Here he threw his spear. Here he sat eating his tripes. And here the corpses were stacked. ...'

Let us hope so.

THE DATING TECHNIQUE

Using an innovative dating technique, we have been able to obtain some dates, which have proved useful in our study of the site at Pelicata.

The dating work referred to in this book has been based upon the development of a revolutionary new dating technique for archaeology, known as *optical thermoluminescence*. It was invented and perfected by our Greek colleague Professor Ioannis Liritzis. Another technique called simply *thermoluminescence*, for dating pottery, and with a somewhat similar name, has been known for a long time. But Ioannis's technique is new, and it dates stone, not pottery.

Until now, it has not been possible for archaeologists to date stone structures directly. All the dates for buildings and structures which you read about are based upon *indirect* methods. Pieces of pottery scattered around a site, or a bit of wood or other organic matter, can be dated. (Wood and organic matter are dated by the well known Carbon 14 method.) Then a conclusion is drawn that perhaps the building is of the same date as the bits and pieces found around or within it. At least the archaeologist hopes so! For what else can he do? He can't date the building itself. Or at least he couldn't until now. Because now it is possible, and everything from now on will change drastically. Instead of the indirect process of 'dating by association', which until today has been practised for all stone buildings and structures, Ioannis can now achieve direct dating of those structures themselves.

Our colleague Professor Ioannis Liritizis was previously a nuclear physicist, and through his knowledge of that field he was able to work out a technique whereby he could calculate the date of the last exposure to light of two pieces of stone which have been pressed together. (I give an explanation of his technique as well as how he developed it in a moment.) Clearly, if we can pinpoint the date when the stones were pressed together for the construction of the building, we have dated the building. Much that was previously guesswork can now become certainty. Although our dating results tend to be spread over several centuries, so that they cannot tell us on their own whether something was built in the reign of a particular king, we can safely classify structures into broader periods of time. In Egypt, for instance, we can say whether something is Old Kingdom, Middle Kingdom, or New Kingdom.

Before he developed his new technique, Ioannis was very familiar with the thermoluminescence method for dating pottery, which he himself used. And he also knew of the OSL (optically stimulated luminescence) dating technique, used especially to date geological sediments, such as marine and fluvial sand and muds, and loess [silt sediment] deposits. Sometimes OSL is used in archaeology, as for instance to date a geological sediment lying over an archaeological site or a burial. It can also be used to date ceramics. OSL dates the time which has elapsed since certain minerals, such as quartz and feldspar, were last exposed to daylight. But no one had ever made use of the concepts underlying this technique to date stone structures.

Ioannis had gone off on his own to try to work out how one might possibly date the walls of a monument directly. He thought about the limestone blocks being cut, and then carved to fit into a wall. He imagined himself being a tiny crystal of limestone experiencing all of this. There he was in his imagination, a 'calcitic crystal', subject to all the environmental stresses which such crystals experience, and he tried to imagine what they were. As a crystal, he absorbed a lot of free electrons from the surrounding radiation of his environment. Some of these came from cosmic rays. Others came from radiation emitted by the radio-isotopes of uranium, thorium, potassium, and rubidium which were in his vicinity, as well as the gamma rays emitted by his environment. (This bombardment is called the 'dose rate', as if the crystal were being forced to swallow medicine.) The crystal which Ioannis had become was heavily-dosed, and had been forced to swallow lots of electrons, which had been squeezed into microscopic holes in the crystal called 'electron traps'. But then suddenly, as a crystal, Ioannis was ripped from the womb of his cozy limestone block and exposed, naked, to the sun. The energy from the sunlight caused all of the electrons to start rushing out of their electron traps, and basically the crystal that Ioannis was started vomiting up all of its medicine. Within only a few hours, the crystal was stripped bare of all of its electrons, and all of its electron traps were empty. Then suddenly, darkness descended, and the crystal was squeezed against another block of limestone, and it never saw the sun again. Slowly, gradually, the electrons returned and began to fill in all the holes once more. But it took a long, long time. The shock of the sunlight, like a cold shower, was never to return, and the traumatized crystal made its way back to normality with a great deal of psychological counselling.

Having experienced all of this as a crystal in his mind, Ioannis had a eureka moment. As he puts it:

'And there was light! An idea came as a striking light! I was inspired! The sunlight exposure had provided the answer.'

Suddenly he realized that the flooding of the limestone crystal with sunlight (which he calls 'bleaching'), and the emptying of its electron traps, could be considered as setting a 'stone clock' to zero. Then when the crystal was covered in darkness again and could begin swallowing its medicine once more, with the electrons creeping in as normal from the ambient radiation, the crystal's clock would be set ticking afresh. And if one removed the crystal again (not exposing it to the light) and counted the electrons which were in it, one could know how many years had elapsed since it had been 'bleached' by the sun. And this would give a date!

Of course there were many details which had to be sorted out as well, such as what kind of environment the stone was in – was it very radioactive or only slightly radioactive (a high dose rate or a low dose rate). That is why Ioannis carries round with him whenever he is collecting samples that extremely heavy machine called a gamma radiation detector, which is such a back-breaker when we go to remote sites!

Plate 18. The remains of the Mycenaean stairway leading up to the site of the Palace. It has been dated to 1430 BC plus or minus 140 years. It is thus approximately 3,500 years old. The level area at its base contains the ruins of the Odysseion Shrine. It is up this stairway that the ancient tourists would have been led by the guides to the site of the ruined Palace. It leads up from the circuit wall to the site, where very few stones now remain visible on the surface. However, these grand stairs are largely intact, although greatly dilapidated, and it was thus possible to take our dating sample which proved the Mycenaean date. We were unable to find anything capable of providing a dating sample higher up, which is an unexcavated area. Future excavations could reveal intact portions of the foundations, from which dating samples could then be taken for further verification. *Photo by Robert Temple.*

Plates 19-20. Additional views of the ancient stairway. (Photos by Robert Temple)

THE DATING RESULTS

Our dating samples at Ithaca were of limestone. As a 'control' for dating purposes, to compare with our result of the Mycenaean stairway, we took a dating sample of the Odysseion/Telemachion just below the palace hill, and it came from the later era, just as we knew it would. The date for this site was 560 BC plus or minus 400 years, giving a range between 960 BC and 160 BC. The earliest possible date for this is therefore two and a half centuries after the collapse of Mycenaean civilisation.

The date which we obtained from the great stairway leading up the hill from this site to what we believe was the Palace of Odysseus on the hilltop was 1430 BC plus or minus 140 years, giving a range between 1570 BC and 1290 BC. In other words, this stairway is clearly of Mycenaean date. It would not have led just to an empty hilltop. We therefore suggest that all the evidence, including the survival of portions of a prominent circuit wall (which we have not dated), points to the hilltop being the location of the great palace. Heurtley's Mycenaean finds associated with the location, combined with our dating result for the stairway, seem to us absolutely conclusive. We look forward to the time when excavations can reveal what we feel confident must remain on the hilltop beneath surface level. A study of Mycenaean stones preserved nearby in other structures would also be most interesting, and if they are merely embedded in terraces, it might be possible to retrieve them and replace them with modern concrete. Certainly, a collection of dispersed original stones brought back to the site would be a useful objective.

THE TEXT(S) OF THE *ODYSSEY*
AND THE OTHER EPICS

We all have our subjective reactions when reading a famous epic such as the *Odyssey*. Mine was very strong: I felt that I was reading an epic poem which had been so heavily altered that it was almost unrecognisable. I felt that it had once had an original form, and that this was not it! It seemed to me that it had been stuffed full of phantasmagoria like a Chekhov play suddenly bringing witches and goblins onstage. For a variety of reasons, some logical and some purely subjective, I became convinced that the original *Odyssey* had been a simple and straightforward saga of the homecoming of Odysseus to Ithaca, which after all takes up such a huge proportion of the epic as it exists today, and is extraordinarily 'normal' (albeit expressed in magnificent poetry) in comparison to the more famous and stranger fantasy episodes which to me seemed to be later intrusions. I had the very strong feeling that the epic had once been called *The Return of Odysseus*. I believe that some later Homeric bard, rather than Homer himself, added the magical and fantasy episodes to Homer's existing epic which had previously been entirely realistic, and devoted only to the return of Odysseus to his home after a long time, and the troubles and perils he had when he arrived there.

What most people today do not realize is that there were many epics about the heroes of the Trojan War in antiquity, not only the two which we still have by Homer, and that the others are lost. The fragments which survive of these lost epics of what is called the Epic Cycle are known as 'Homerica' and are to be found in the Loeb Library volume *Hesiod, The Homeric Hymns, and Homerica* of 1982,[50] and in its expanded successor volume of 2003, from which Hesiod is excluded and more Homerica included, *Greek Epic Fragments*.[51] There was even more than one *Iliad*!

The entire Trojan story was told in a series of eight separate epic poems, only two of which, the *Iliad* and the *Odyssey*, now survive in their entirety. Where one epic ended the next commenced. The series began with an epic called the *Cypria*, which was fairly long ('eleven books', nearly half the length of the *Odyssey*, which is in 24 books), which described the circumstances leading up to the Trojan War, including the abduction of Helen. It was written by Stasinus of Cyprus, or perhaps by Hegesinus of Salamis; their dates are unknown, but may have been the seventh or eighth centuries BC. According to the Byzantine author John Tzetses, this book was really written by Homer but inherited by Stasinus, who put his name on it and claimed it as his own work.[52] A lengthy summary of this work, plus 31 fragments, are preserved in the Homerica. One curious detail recorded in the *Cypria* informs us that it took only three days for Paris and Helen to sail from Sparta to Troy, enjoying a favourable wind. This is an extraordinary contrast with the many years of roaming over the sea of the returning heroes afterwards! This detail is especially commented upon by Herodotus in his *History*. After mentioning that Homer had said that when Paris (also called Alexander) had abducted Helen, he made a diversion to Egypt on his way home to Troy, he refers to the *Cypria* and uses this as evidence that the *Cypria* could not have been written by Homer:

'… the *Cypria* is not by Homer but by someone else. For in the *Cypria* it is stated that Alexander [Paris] arrived from Sparta at Ilion [Troy] with Helen on the third day, having had a fair wind and a smooth sea, whereas in the *Iliad* he says that he went on a diversion with her.'[53]

The Iliad of Homer was the next in the sequence. Next after that was the epic called the *Aethiopis*, written by Arctinus of Miletus, who was known to be alive in 776 BC. It was less than half the length of the *Cypria*, being only 'five books'. Part of the action of this epic overlapped with that of the *Iliad*. A summary of this book and only six fragments survive in the Homerica.

The next epic in the sequence was the brief *Little Iliad*, only two books long, but we have a summary plus 32 fragments of this work in the Homerica. This short epic was written by Lesches (or Lescheos), son of Aeschylinos, who lived about 660 BC. He came from a small village on the island of Lesbos named Pyrhha (a strange name, meaning 'red-head'; this site on the northeast shore of the Kolpos Kallonis is now underwater because of an earthquake), which in antiquity was largely inhabited by fishermen. It was in this village, and probably either in the actual house of Lesches, or otherwise in a more recent house on its site (the place was too small to have many substantial dwellings!), where Aristotle lived for some time when he was studying fish for his zoological researches. Aristotle would have been well aware of the fact that he was living in the home village of the author of the *Little Iliad*, a work which he mentions in his *Poetics*, showing that he had made a particularly close study of it, and he even criticised it for being too diffuse and not concentrating on a unified theme:

'We have proof of Homer's marvellous superiority to the rest ⌈of the authors of the other Trojan epics⌉. …whereas the *Iliad* or *Odyssey* supplies materials for only one, or at most two tragedies, the *Cypria* does that for several and the *Little Iliad* for more than eight …'[54]

Next in the series was another lost epic called *The Sack of Troy*, or *The Sack of Ilium*, of which a summary and five fragments survive. Pausanius (second century AD) said that this epic too was written by Lesches/Lescheos.[55] However, we know from ancient comments that both this work and the *Little Iliad* duplicated each other to a certain extent. Ingram Bywater convincingly suggests that what survives of *the Sack of Troy* is not from a separate work at all, but is really 'the concluding part of the *Little Iliad* under another name'.[56] He says the *Little Iliad*, from the summary we have of it, ends too abruptly, and certainly I would add to his comments that the epic by Lesches must have been more than only two books long in order to contain the eight separate tragic stories which Aristotle ascribes to it. So, on this basis, there would originally have been only seven Trojan epics to the Epic Cycle, which later became eight when the text of the *Little Iliad* was split into two after the time of Aristotle, possibly by a manuscript breaking apart or the sequences of book rolls being separated and jumbled up, resulting in the work being mistakenly catalogued in a library, such as that at Alexandria, as two separate works.

There is another tradition that an epic called *The Sack of Troy* was composed by Demodocus of Corcyra, information which was preserved by Plato's colleague Heraclides of Pontus. He was discussed earlier. Were there therefore two works concerning *the sack of Troy*? Demodocus appears in person in the *Odyssey*, where Odysseus himself asks him to sing of *the sack of Troy*. But, as described earlier, there was independent information about Demodocus apart from what is said of him in the *Odyssey*. We shall probably never know the answers to the many questions which arise about these matters.

The vivid descriptions of the sack of Troy given in the above epics (or epic, if they were the same work) were the inspiration for the similar scenes described with such power by Vergil in his *Aeneid*. Indeed, in writing the *Aeneid*, Vergil was really taking the daring step of adding another Trojan epic to the existing Greek Epic Cycle, to demonstrate that the Romans could match the Greeks at that kind of thing. It was what we would today call *making a statement*.

The next epic in the cycle was called *The Returns*, which was five books long and written by Agias (or Hegias) of Troezen, of whom nothing is known. A summary and thirteen fragments survive. The alternative title of this work was *The Return of the Atreidae*, referring to Agamemnon and Menelaus, the most prominent of the Greeks, who were known as 'the sons of Atreus'. It is known that this work described the return to their homes after the Trojan War of all the leading Greeks except Odysseus, whom it only mentioned once in passing. It is believed therefore that *The Returns* was written to supplement the *Odyssey*, which fully describes Odysseus's return. But if so, I believe that the *Odyssey* which it supplemented was not the *Odyssey* which we know today, but was instead a simple and straightforward *Return of Odysseus*. The existence of this other major epic of *Returns* strikes me as a confirmation of this hypothesis. *The Returns* was not written to provide more Calypsos and more Cyclops, it was written to describe the returns of the other Greeks, the emphasis being very much on the 'return home' motif. The reason why I have gone into this at such length is to make this point, and to stress that I believe that all aspects of the *Odyssey* which concern the return to Ithaca itself are extraordinarily reliable, and careful about detail. They should not be dismissed as fantasy in the way we can easily dismiss many of the details of the magical episodes. This is important for us in our consideration of the Palace of Odysseus.

The next epic in the series was the *Odyssey* itself. And the Epic Cycle then drew to a close with the final epic in the series, *The Telegony*, which was a poem of only two books written by Eugammon of Cyrene, who was alive in 568 BC. It took up the story where the *Odyssey* left off, and commenced with the dead suitors being buried by their kinsmen. The main theme of this epic was Telegonus ('the one born far off'), the son of Odysseus by either Circe or, as was occasionally maintained (such as mistakenly by Eustathius),[57] of Calypso, who ends up by marrying his step-mother Penelope after he has killed his father by mistake! According to this epic, in between the death of the suitors and his return long afterwards to Ithaca, Odysseus went and settled in Thesprotia, in northwestern Greece not far from Ithaca, and married its queen, by whom he had a son Polypoetes, who became King of Thesprotia upon her death. After this, the long-suffering Penelope was still waiting for him at home so Odysseus returned to her once more, but it is not surprising that with such a feckless husband, she ended up marrying a younger man who had killed him (albeit it was his own father) and starting again. And so ends the cycle …!

At the very least, Aristotle was in agreement nearly two and a half millennia ago with my own attitude towards this matter of the integrity of the epic! He did know the fantasy elements, since he refers to the conflict between Odysseus and Polyphemus in his *Rhetoric*.[58] However, Aristotle chose to ignore these episodes when discussing the *Odyssey per se*. This may be because the Ionian Islands version of the *Odyssey* was purely a *Return of Odysseus*, so that it may have been clear to Aristotle that the magical episodes were all interpolations. There is an interesting book dealing with what Aristotle did know about Homer's works, entitled *The Homer of Aristotle*.[59] This book reveals among other things that the *Iliad* and the *Odyssey* contained cryptogram prefaces, like the works of the dramatists and other epic poets, an important subject which I have already discussed in an earlier book, so I shall not repeat the discussion here.[60]

Aristotle's association with the Homeric texts was extraordinarily extensive and deep. We know that he even prepared a special edition of *The Iliad* personally. This information is recorded by the famous historian Plutarch, who in his *Life of Alexander* (Chapter 8) tells us:

'He (Alexander the Great) was likewise fond of literature and of reading, and we are told by Onesicritos that he was wont to call the *Iliad* a complete manual of the military art, and that he always carried with him Aristotle's recension of the poem, called *The Iliad* of the Casket, and always kept it lying with his dagger under his pillow.'[61]

As to the reason why Aristotle's recension of *The Iliad* was called 'the casket copy', this is explained also by Plutarch:

'When a small casket was brought to him, which those in charge of the [seized] baggage and wealth of Darius [the defeated Persian Emperor] thought the most precious thing there, he asked his friends what valuable object they thought would most fittingly be deposited in it. And when many answered and there were many opinions, Alexander himself said he was going to deposit the *Iliad* there for safe keeping.'[62]

And as the author Strabo adds:

'... we are told of a recension of the poetry of Homer, the *Recension of the Casket*, as it is called, which Alexander, along with Callisthenes [the nephew of Aristotle] and Anaxarchus, perused and to a certain extent annotated, and then deposited in a richly wrought casket which he had found amongst the Persian treasures.'[63]

These testimonies are unmistakable proof that Aristotle personally prepared new critical editions of Homer. Alexander kept Aristotle's edition of *The Iliad* under his pillow in a bejewelled casket captured from the Emperor Darius. *The Odyssey* may have been with it. But in any case, we know from the evidence already given that Aristotle had collected the Ithacan version of *The Odyssey*, presumably at the same time that he visited the island in pursuit of materials for the composition of his now lost *Constitution of Ithaca*, one of 158 constitutions of Greek city states which he collected and published. It is difficult to know what effect Aristotle's work on the Homeric texts had on what has survived to modern times. He also wrote an extended learned commentary in ten books, *Questions Relating to Recondite Problems in the Poetry of Homer*, which is now lost, but which may have had a major effect on the post-Aristotelian editions of Homer, and hence on those versions which we have today. The book was certainly on deposit in the Alexandrian Library before it burned down.[64]

Plutarch in his work *Greek Questions* preserves some further information which is of interest to us. This work is found in the collection of writings by Plutarch commonly known as the *Moralia*, which are greater in bulk than his *Lives*, and which are of unending fascination on just about every question under the sun. In Chapter 14 of *Greek Questions*, Plutarch gives some curious information about Odysseus which appears to have been discussed and preserved by Aristotle in his lost work which has just been mentioned. This passage is ignored by Sir David Ross, who may not have known of it, when he compiled the volume of Aristotelian Fragments in translation as part of the Oxford *Works of Aristotle*.[65] I quote the entire chapter, which is brief, from the wonderful Elizabethan translation by Philemon Holland, as his translations of various classical works are some of the most fascinating examples of the English language at its richest stage, and I have all of these translations in old leather folio volumes which I greatly treasure and frequently read over and over again:

'Who be those inhabitants of Ithaca, named Colliades? And who is Phagilus among them?

'After that Ulysses [Odysseus] had killed those who wooed his wife in his absence, the kinsfolke and friends of them being now dead, rose up against him to be revenged:

but in the end they agreed on both sides to send for Neoptolemus, to make an accord and atonement betweene them: who having undertaken this arbitrement [arbitration], awarded that Ulysses should depart out of those parts, and quit the Isles of Cephalenia [now called Cephallonia], Ithaca, and Zacynthus, in regard of the bloudshed that he had committed. Item, that the kinsfolke and friends of the said wooers should pay a certaine fine every year unto Ulysses in recompence for the riot, damage, and havock they had made in his house. As for Ulysses, he withdrew himselfe and departed into Italy: but for the mulct or fine imposed upon them, which he had consecrated unto the gods; he took order that those of Ithaca should tender the payment thereof unto his son [Telemachus, who reigned as king after his father exiled himself]: and the same was a quantity of meale and of wine, a certaine number of wax-lights [candles made of beeswax] or tapers. Oyle, salt, and for sacrifices the bigger sort and better grown of Phagili: now Phagilus, Aristotle interpreteth to be a lambe.

'Moreover, as touching Eumaeus [the royal swineherd, Odysseus's old friend, who helped him slay the suitors], Telemachus enfranchised him and all his posterity [i.e. gave them freemen status as citizens of Ithaca, freeing them from servant status]; yea, and endued them with the right of free bourgeosie [so that they could take part in political assemblies]. And so the progeny of Eumaeus are at this day the house and family called Coliadae ...'[66]

Phagilos does indeed mean 'lamb', as Aristotle said, specifically 'a lamb ready for eating', as Liddell & Scott's *Greek Lexicon* makes clear, citing Aristotle's Fragment 464 (Rose), the passage we have just read, and also pointing out the variant spellings and that the later Greek dictionary compiler Hesychius of Alexandria of the fifth century AD recorded the same meaning, as did Eustathius (1625.38), who lived in the fourth century AD. If Plutarch were alive today, he would be delighted to get this fuller answer to this particular 'Greek Question' of his.

The way in which Plutarch presents all of this information makes it unmistakeable that it all comes from Aristotle, and undoubtedly a section of his *Homeric Questions* dealing with Ithaca. The story of what happened to Odysseus and Telemachus after the story of the *Odyssey* is far too detailed to be a myth. Aristotle appears to have collected this information during his visit to the Ionian Islands, either as verbal tradition or more likely from some local history. Local histories definitely did exist in classical antiquity, but none has survived except for rare fragments quoted by more general authors and historians. One example which is well documented is *The History of Delos*, written as a local history by a native author of Delos named Semus. It is quoted several times by the later author Athenaeus (lived second-third century AD), who evidently possessed a copy of this rare book in his personal library.[67] Such works by local historians, of which there must have been many, were gobbled up by more cosmopolitan historians, absorbed into their works, but rarely explicitly cited, and the works themselves were lost. The tradition that Odysseus lived at some point in his life in southwest Italy is well known, and has been discussed in numerous books and articles. Many locations there today are said to derive their names from Odyssean connections. For instance, Baia is said to have been named after Baios, a companion of Odysseus. However, his name does not appear in the *Odyssey*, so he comes from another epic or another tradition altogether. Monte Circeo on the western coast of Italy is said to have been associated with the character Circe in the *Odyssey*. I should point out that the tradition that Odysseus went to live on Thesprotia on the mainland of Greece, and then returned to Ithaca and was murdered, as described in the brief but late epic The *Telegony* by Eugammon of Cyrene in Libya (alive 568 BC), which was discussed above, is not in agreement with the Ithacan tradition that Odysseus migrated to southwest Italy. W. R. Halliday said in the notes to his modern translation of Plutarch's *Greek Questions*:

'The version [of the story], then, which Aristotle was following, is markedly different not only from Homer [as conventionally known] but from the Cyclic tradition [the Epic Cycle], and a feature of it seems to be a relatively local interest. The places and persons belong to North-Western Greece and its islands. … Now that a local version of the story of Odysseus existed which differed from the epic tradition precisely in respect of the localization of persons and characters in the vicinity of Ithaka, and further that is was known to Aristotle, seems to be shown by [Aristotle's] *Poetics*, xxv, 16, 1461b … the Kephallenian [Cephallonian] story may perhaps be the true one. They allege that Odysseus took a wife from among themselves … I am inclined, therefore, to think that the version of Odysseus's adventures which was followed by Aristotle … had its origin in the Ionian islands.'[68]

There is another important thing to mention here, which is that there was a tradition recorded by Aristotle's contemporary, Heraclides of Pontus, that some of the 'Homeric' material was composed by a native of Ithaca named Phemius. He is specifically described as having 'composed a *Return of the Heroes* who set out from Troy with Agamemnon'.[69] This would certainly have been known by Aristotle, who was a colleague of Heraclides, and we can be sure that he discussed it in his own lost writings about the Homeric works. Phemius, son of Terpios, is actually mentioned in Book One of the *Odyssey* as a bard of Ithaca who was alive at the time of Odysseus. Just after Telemachus has finished his conversation with the goddess Athena, disguised as a seafaring visitor named Mentes, Lord of the Taphians, he returns to a feast being held by the wooers of his mother. And we are told:

'For them the famous minstrel [Phemius] was singing, and they sat in silence listening; and he sang of the Achaeans – the woeful return from Troy which Pallas Athene has laid upon them. And from her upper chamber the daughter of Icarius, wise Penelope, heard his wondrous song, and she went down the high stairway from her chamber, not alone, for two handmaids attended her. Now when the fair lady had come to the wooers, she stood by the doorpost of the well-built hall, holding before her face her shining veil; and a faithful handmaid stood on either side of her. Then she burst into tears, and spoke to the divine minstrel:

'"Phemius, many other things thou knowest to charm mortals, deeds of men and gods which minstrels make famous. Sing them one of these, as thou sittest here, and let them drink their wine in silence. But cease from this woeful song which ever harrows my heart in my breast, for upon me above all women has come a sorrow not to be forgotten. So dear a head do I ever remember with longing, even my husband, whose fame is wide through Hellas and mid-Argos."'

But her son Telemachus asks her not to begrudge the bard his wish to sing whatever is in his heart and says: '"With this man no one can be wroth if he sings of the evil doom of the Danaans; for men praise that song the most which comes the newest to their ears."'[70]

We have thus a strange situation, where the *Odyssey* specifically informs us that a bard named Phemius of Ithaca had already just composed an epic poem ('which comes newest to their ears') about the return of the Greeks from Troy, other than Odysseus himself, just prior to the return of Odysseus. We should not dismiss this as a fanciful element of the tale. Instead, it appears to be testimony to the existence of an epic called *The Returns* which was so old that it was already known to the inhabitants of Ithaca in

Mycenaean times, and that it had been composed by the Ithacan bard named Phemius, of whom nothing else is known. Both Heraclides of Pontus and the unknown author of a treatise entitled *On Music* believed that Phemius existed and that he composed an epic about *The Returns*. This appears to have been accepted by the many authors on the history of music cited in the treatise *On Music*, whose works constituted an enormous literature which is now entirely lost. It is thus possible that there was more than one epic concerning *The Returns*. Indeed, the subject was possibly sung by bards all over Hellas across the many centuries. There is no need for us to think that there was only ever a single epic of *The Returns*. There may have been many. Most of these would have been lost long before classical times, and never written down at all, having been held only in the bardic memories of a class of wandering minstrels who had ceased to exist, taking their poems with them to the grave. Indeed, it may well have been in hopes of finding manuscripts in Ithaca which were unknown at Athens that took Aristotle to Ithaca, a trip handy for him in that it also enabled him to collect copies of the local constitutions at the same time, which were included in his famous collection of 158 constitutions, of which only one, that of Athens, survives today. (And Aristotle's *Constitution of Athens* itself was only recovered from a papyrus found in Egypt at the end of the 19th century.) I have already mentioned that there was more than one *Iliad*, so it is not unlikely that there was more than one *Returns*. In fact, when you think about it, every successful bard of Greece may well have had his own version of one or more of what we call 'the Homerica'. These were the foundation legends of Greece, so how could anyone of those days call himself a bard if he could not recite or sing at least one epic about them? And each bard would feel free to add his own variations, just as pianists add their own cadenzas to keyboard music today.

The recovery of some lost texts from charred papyri discovered in the Villa of the Papyri at Herculaneum has led to a bit more light being shed on this subject. The texts recovered and published so far from the villa at Herculaneum have largely been by the Epicurean philosopher Philodemus. Richard Janko, who has had a lifelong interest in the writings of Aristotle on literature and poetry, has edited the three volumes of Philodemus *On Poets*,[71] and the volume which concerns us is the last one, which was published in 2011. Because of its relation to the main contents of the volume, he decided to add at the end of that volume the surviving fragments of Aristotle's lost work *On Poets*. (This should not be confused with Aristotle's separate work *The Poetics*.) In these fragments we learn more about both Homer and the Homerica. Both Aristotle and Heraclides of Pontus insisted that Homer had been born on the island of Ios. During his lifetime, Homer had a rival and 'enemy', Syagrus, who 'competed with Homer' (as a bard). And according to a fragment of Aristotle's lost work preserved by Aelian: 'Syagrus ... is said to have been the first to sing of the Trojan War, getting hold of a very great subject and venturing upon it'.[72] We must take this information seriously, since it comes from Aristotle and Heraclides. As regards Aristotle's information that Homer came from Ios, he specifically stated that 'the people of Ios relate that Homer was born to a spirit who danced with the Muses'. He quotes the inscription upon Homer's tomb at Ios: 'Here doth the earth the holy head conceal/ of godlike Homer, marshaller of heroes.' These and other details communicated by Aristotle strongly suggest that Aristotle had visited Ios in person, doubtless acquiring a copy of its constitution and information about Homer at the same time, as he did at Ithaca. Aristotle also records that Timotheus of Miletus, a 5th century BC bard at the Court of Macedon who must have been known to Aristotle's father when he was the royal physician there, had written a 'lament of Odysseus'.[73]

And Marcion preserves this information about Aristotle's connection with Homer:

'As long as he (Aristotle) was still young, he was educated in the liberal arts, as is clear from the *Homeric Questions* that he wrote, the edition of the *Iliad* which he gave to Alexander, his dialogue *On Poets*, and his *Handbooks on Rhetoric*.'[74]

This same information is given also by another author:

'When Aristotle was still young, he was trained in the liberal arts, as is clear from his writings *On Poetics* and *Regarding Poets*, and again his *Homeric Problems* and *Handbooks on Rhetoric*.'[75]

Another important point made by the scholar Richard Janko in an article in 1998[76] concerns the fact that both the *Iliad* and the *Odyssey* as well as all the other epic poems were, as most scholars would agree, originally oral compositions of the travelling bards. But he points out that as the bards travelled around, they would have varied their tales to match popular taste and please the local king at whose court they were reciting. An *Odyssey* which was primarily focused on Ithacan and Cephallonian tradition would inevitably have had some variations made by the bard when recited far away from Ithaca, so that another version would come into existence. And it is not unlikely that there were many such varying versions. As Janko points out, someone with a great deal of wealth such as a king would have had to commission the writing down of the *Odyssey* and the *Iliad* on numerous leather rolls, a task which would have taken weeks or months. Since the scribes doing this would be doing that particular version, that is the one that would have become 'standard'. Perhaps because he realized this, Aristotle sought earlier materials in Ithaca, where he suspected the most authentic version would be found.

It is obvious that this discovery of the site of the Palace of Odysseus could eventually be of great benefit to the tourist industry of Greece, though we hope that the tranquil quality of Ithaca will not be ruined by its announcement. However, considering the worldwide heritage represented by the story of Odysseus, people who value the origins of Western culture and may have, for instance, visited the site of Troy or the Palace of Mycenae, should have the opportunity of visiting also the site of this palace, and some efforts should be made to uncover whatever remains of it so that the reality of what for so long has been legend can be seen once again by all.

ENDNOTES

1   Charles Albert Savage, *The Athenian Family: A Sociological and Legal Study Based Chiefly on the Works of the Attic Orators*, Baltimore, 1907. This was his privately published Ph.D. thesis for Johns Hopkins University. Until recent years, it was essentially unknown. I had an original copy and nearly persuaded my friend Colin Haycraft to publish it as a Duckworth title, but he backed out. At last it is now available in a modern reprint edition.

2   *Ibid.*, pp. 102-3.

3   Halliday, W. R., *The Greek Questions of Plutarch with a New Translation & a Commentary*, Clarendon Press, Oxford, 1928, pp. 79-81.

4   Aristotle, *op. cit.*, 1455b, 16-23.

5   Farnell, Lewis Richard, *Greek Hero Cults and Ideas of Immortality*, Oxford, 1921, p. 326.

6   Platthy, *op. cit.*, pp. 109-110. The epigram is preserved in the *Palatine Anthology* XI, 442; T 15.

7   Heurtley, W. A., 'The Site of the Palace of Odysseus', in *Antiquity*, Volume IX, Number 36, December, 1935, pp. 410-417.

8   *Ibid.*, p. 410.

9   Halliday, *op. cit.*, p. 79 (Greek Question 14).

10   Nilsson, Martin, *The Mycenaean Origin of Greek Mythology*, Sather Classical Lectures, Volume 8, University of California Press, Berkeley, California, USA, 1932, pp. 95-98.

11   Heurtley, *op. cit.*, pp. 416-7.

12   Aristotle, *Rhetoric*, Book II, 22, 12, *op. cit.*, pp. 293-5.

13   *Op. cit.*, the first two chapters.

14   Page, Denys, *The Homeric Odyssey*, Clarendon Press, Oxford, 1955, pp. 138-9.

15   Homer, *The Odyssey*, Book VIII, 254 – 586.

16   'Plutarch' (Pseudo-Plutarch), *On Music*, 1132 B, translated jointly by Benedict Einarson and Phillip H. de Lacy, in Volume XIV of the series of Plutarch's *Moralia*, Harvard University Press, 1967, pp. 358-8.

17   *The Peri Mousikēs of Plutarch*, translated by the Rev. John Healy Bromby, privately printed at Chiswick, England, 1822, p. 11. I am fortunate to have an inscribed copy of this rare book presented to Bromby's friend Edward Wilson. Loosely inserted into the volume was an original letter from Bromby to his friend and patron, to whom he had officially dedicated the book, John Broadley. Both men died tragically early, Bromby at the age of 37 (in 1830) and Broadley at the age of 48 (in 1833); they had originally met when young in Kingston upon Hull.

18   Andrew Barker, *Greek Musical Writings, Volume I, The Musician and His Art*, Cambridge University Press, 1984, p. 207.

19   Chroust, Anton-Hermann, *Aristotle: New Light on His Life and on Some of His Lost Works*, 2 vols., Routledge & Kegan Paul, London, 1973, Vol., I, p. 93.

20   Homer, *The Odyssey*, translated by Robert Fitzgerald, Heinemann, London, 1962, p. 221.

21   *Ibid.*, p. 271.

22   *Ibid.*, p. 270.

23   *Ibid.*, p. 283.

24   *Ibid.*

25   *Ibid.*, p. 284.

26   *Ibid.*, p. 286.

27   *Ibid.*, p. 289.

28   *Ibid.*, p. 302.

29   *Ibid.*, p. 295.

30   *Ibid.*, pp. 319-20 give details of sheepskins spread on chairs and benches.

31   *Ibid.*, p. 308.

32   *Ibid.*, p. 298.

33   *Ibid.*, p. 318.

34   *Ibid.*, p. 305.

35   *Ibid.*, p. 319.

36   Lorimer, H. L., *Homer and the Monuments*, Macmillan, London, 1950, p. 416.

37   *Odyssey, op. cit.*, p. 345.

38   *Ibid.*, p. 358.

39   *Ibid.*, pp. 371-2.

40   *Ibid.*, p. 378.

41   *Ibid.*, pp. 381-2.

42   *Ibid.*, p. 386.

43   *Ibid.*, p. 390.

44   Rider, Bertha Carr, *The Greek House*, Cambridge University Press, original edition 1916, reprinted 1965.

45   *Ibid.*, pp. 166-209.

46   Halliday, *op. cit.*, pp. 81-2, for the Telemachos aspect, and p. 194 for cults and shrines (one even oracular) of Odysseus at Ithaca and elsewhere.

47   *Ibid.*, p. 81.

48   *Odyssey, op. cit.*, p. 306.

49   *Ibid.*, pp. 318-9.

50   *Hesiod, The Homeric Hymns, and Homerica*, translated by H. G. Evelyn-White, Loeb Library Series, Harvard University Press, USA, 1982.

51   *Greek Epic Fragments*, edited and translated by Martin L. West, Loeb Library Series, Harvard University Press, USA, 2003.

52   1982 edition., p. 497. In the 2003 edition, p. 67, this information is shown to have been preserved by Photius; West discusses the matter on p. 13. He also points out that Pindar already knew the story that the *Cypria* had been composed by Homer and given to a man named Stasinus as dowry for his daughter. Both Photius and Aelian repeated this story, which was well-known in antiquity, though that is no guarantee of its being true.

53   The 2003 edition of *Greek Epic Fragments*, pp. 95-7.

54   Aristotle, *Poetics*, Chapter 23, 1459a-b, translated by Sir David Ross, *The Works of Aristotle*, Volume XI, Clarendon Press, Oxford, 1966.

55   Pausanius, *Description of Greece*, Book Ten, 25, 26, and 27, translated with commentary by (Sir) James G. Frazer, 6 vols., Macmillan, London, 1913, Vol. I and commentary in Vol. V. See particularly Vol. V, pp. 362-3.

56   Bywater, Ingram, translator and extensive commentator, *Aristotle on the Art of Poetry*, Clarendon Press, Oxford, 1909, p. 309.

57   *Hesiod,... Homerica*, 1982, *op. cit.*, pp. 532-3, and in the 2003 edition, this is found at p. 171 (and see the footnote); Eusthatius says the mother of Telegonus was Circe, and that Telegonus was also known as Teledamus.

58   Aristotle, *Rhetoric*, Book II, Chapter 3, 16, translation by J. H. Freese, Loeb Library Series, Harvard University Press, USA, 1994, p. 191.

59   Margoliouth, D. S., *The Homer of Aristotle*, Blackwell, Oxford, 1923.

60   Temple, Robert, *Netherworld*, Century, London, 2002, pp. 17-19; pp. 20-22 of paperback edition (Arrow, London, 2002). The updated American edition is entitled *Oracles of the Dead*, Inner Traditions International, Rochester, Vermont, U.S.A., 2005.

61   Plutarch, 'Life of Alexander', Chapter 8, 2. My amendment of the translation by Aubrey Stewart and George Long, in *Plutarch's Lives*, 4 vols., Bohns Library, London, 1889, Vol. III, pp. 306-7.

62   Plutarch, 'Life of Alexander', Chapter 26, 1. Translation by Bernadotte Perrin, in *Plutarch's Lives*, Loeb Classical Library, Harvard University Press, USA, Vol. VII, p. 299.

63   Jeno Platthy, *Sources on the Earliest Greek Libraries with the Testimonia*, Hakkert, Amsterdam, 1968, p. 141.

64   *Ibid.*, p. 126, information drawn from an Arabic source, which drew upon Ptolemy's lost *Life of Aristotle*. The bibliographical list of Aristotle's works preserved by Diogenes Laertius describes this work as being in six books, and gives it the title *Homeric Problems*: see *Diogenes Laertius*, Loeb Classical Library, Harvard University Press, USA, 2 vols., Vol. I, p. 473. In this instance, Ptolemy as cited by the Arabs is more likely to be correct.

65   Ross, Sir David, *The Works of Aristotle*, Clarendon Press, Oxford, 12 vols., 1952, Volume XII: *Select Fragments*. The one in question was either not selected or not known to Ross.

66   Plutarch, *Greek Questions*, Chapter 14, translated under the title *Questions as touching Greek affaires*, by Philemon Holland in the volume *The Philosophy Commonly Called the Morals Written by the Learned Philosopher Plutarch*, London, revised second edition of 1657, p. 730.

67   Athenaeus, *The Deipnosophists or Banquet of the Learned*, translated by C. D. Yonge, Bohns Library, London and New York, 1854, 3 vols., pp. 50, 62, 181, 203, 524, 747, 979, 985, 986, 992, 1018, 1030, 1031, 1208. There is also a more recent Loeb Library translation of Athenaeus.

68   Halliday, *op. cit.*, pp. 80-1.

69   This information, stated as having been taken from Heraclides of Pontus, is found in the treatise *On Music*, often attributed to Plutarch, but really by another unknown author, whom we shall call Pseudo-Plutarch. It appears however in the Loeb Library series of the *Moralia* of Plutarch, Volume XIV, translated jointly by Benedict Einarson and Phillip H. de Lacy, Harvard University Press, 1967, pp. 358-9. This fragment of the lost writings of Heraclides of Pontus is labeled Fragment 157 by F. Wehrli, the editor.

70   Homer, *The Odyssey*, Book One, 323-355, translated by A. T. Murray, Loeb Library, Harvard University Press, 1919, pp. 26-29.

71   Philodemus, *On Poems*, Books Three and Four, *with the Fragments of Aristotle On Poets*, edited and translated by Richard Janko, Oxford University Press, 2011; two previous volumes of this work were also edited and translated by Richard Janko.

72   *Ibid.*, pp. 474-477.

73   *Ibid.*, pp. 468-469.(Information preserved by Aristocles of Messene.)

74   *Ibid.*, pp. 412-413. (From Marcion's *Life of Aristotle*.)

75   *Ibid.* (From Vulgate *Life of Aristotle*.)

76   Richard Janko, 'The Homeric Poems as Oral Dictated Texts', in *The Classical Quarterly*, New Series, Volume 42, Number 1, 1998, pp. 1-13. The tradition of the Homeric tests being oral compositions is well attested, and has been discussed many times, but it is not our purpose here to survey the history of those discussions; some key references are to be found in Janko's paper.

Figure 21 Odysseus seated on a rock with a sword in his hand, with which he has just sacrificed two sheep. His name is written in front of his face in capital letters. (The ancient Greeks did not use lower case Greek letters, which were invented by modern people.) Around his neck hangs his wayfarer's hat. This is a detail of a larger scene of Odysseus visiting the Oracle of the Dead and summoning up from Hades the spirit of his dead friend Elpenor, at whom he is gazing. From a two-handled ceramic pelike vase painting in Boston.